Table of Contents

It's Time To Change Your Life For The Better

"The first step towards getting somewhere is to decide that you are not going to stay where you are"
Chauncey Depew

You have probably picked up this book because you are struggling with issues of confidence and self-esteem. So let me start by saying well done for taking an important step towards helping yourself. You are the only one who can do that. Everyone needs encouragement, particularly at the start of a journey like this, so let's look at some motivating facts to spur you on.

First of all, you are ***not*** alone. Google the phrase *"successful people with low self-confidence"* and you will come back with 29,800,000 results. There are websites and blogs galore about talented individuals from all walks of life who either had self-confidence issues when they were young or have battled low self-esteem all their lives. Award-winning British movie actress Kate Winslet, whose big break came in 1997 when she was cast as Rose in the blockbuster Titanic alongside Leonardo DiCaprio, is a prime example of someone who has overcome self-doubt to become hugely successful.

She dedicated her 2016 BAFTA for Best Supporting Actress to *"all the young women who doubt themselves because you shouldn't be doubting. You should just be going for it."* Winslet recalled how, at the age of just 14, a drama teacher told her *"I might do okay if I was happy to settle for the fat girl parts."*

This brutal advice, if advice is the right word, could have broken her, but instead she resolved not to conform to anyone else's idea of perfection. *"What I feel like saying in those moments is any young woman who has ever been put down by a teacher, a friend, or even a parent: Just don't listen to it, because that's what I did. I didn't listen, and I kept on going and I overcame my fears and a lot of insecurity."*

Winslet recently addressed a group of 12,000 school pupils at the WE Day UK celebrations in London. She told them how she was bullied at school, nicknamed Blubber, locked in a cupboard, laughed at for wanting to be an actress and for having big feet and not being the prettiest. At the end of her inspirational speech she told her audience: *"you can be from anywhere, and you CAN do anything. Believe it. I learned to embrace my flaws, to make no apology for who I am."*

Can You Be TOO Confident?

Back in 2012, Harvard Business Review published an article on self-confidence by Professor of Business Psychology at University College, London, Tomas Chamorro- Premuzic. Nothing new about that, you might think. People are always banging on about the need to assert yourself in order to get on in life, climb the career ladder, have a brilliant relationship, yada, yada, yada.

This article was different, though. The title was ***Less-Confident People are More Successful***. I bet *that* made you pay attention! Professor Chamorro-Premuzic made the case for low self-confidence and how those whose egos are not the size of a small planet are actually far more likely to achieve their goals and turn in stellar performances. He attributed this to three things.

First, those with low self-confidence are likely to be more self-critical and pay attention to negative feedback. As he says, *"to be the very best at anything, you will need to be your harshest critic, and that is almost impossible to achieve when your starting point is high self-confidence."*

Second, if you are serious about your goals then a lack of confidence in your own abilities means you are more likely to work hard to overcome your perceived shortcomings. In the lovely Prof's opinion, this is far better than breezing along thinking your natural brilliance will be dazzling enough to see you through.

Third, you are not going to be a deluded and ego-centric narcissist who is hated at work and loathed outside it. Despite the current obsession with celebrities, selfies and reality TV, it turns out that people actually don't like those with over-inflated opinions of themselves. Shocker.

What is the moral of this? That where you are right now is a good starting point to achieve great things, and also that you need to have the right amount of self-confidence. Not too high, but not too low either. In fact, Chamorro-Premuzic makes it very clear in his article that he is not talking about extremely low confidence, which is *"not helpful, it inhibits performance by inducing fear, worry and stress"*, but rather *"just-low-enough."* So that is what we are going to work towards. Getting you to a healthy and helpful level of self-confidence and assertiveness.

How This Book Will Help Your Life

By reading this far, you have proved that you are serious

about working on your self-confidence. That's great. It means that you are ready for change and ready to try out some new ideas. It will take some work, but together we **will** get there. The alternative is to stay where you are, and that is a decision you are free to take, of course. But before you stick with the status quo, do yourself a favor and read the book. You may be surprised at what you learn.

We will begin by looking at the background to confidence, fear and assertiveness. After all, you need to fully understand what you are aiming towards and what you need to avoid. We will also be looking at your biggest and most under-rated asset. Your mind. You will learn how tremendously powerful it is and how to make it work for you, rather than against you. Shakespeare's character Hamlet puts it very well: *"for there is nothing either good or bad, but thinking makes it so."* Good old Shakespeare, he's really hit the nail on the head there!

Once we have established the foundations, we will begin to rebuild your confidence, using a series of strategies which you can try out. You may not need them all, you may not like them all, but there will definitely be a few which will strike home. Think of what you learn in this book like your own personal self-confidence toolkit, there for you to select from and use as the need arises.

Although it deals with a serious subject, this is going to be a light-hearted book which I hope you will enjoy using. Laughter is so important, not just in building self-esteem, but in life. And you are more likely to remember and keep using techniques if they are fun.

By the time you have finished reading, you should be fully equipped to deal confidently with situations you used to dread. You will have a number of different strategies to cope with life's slings and arrows (sorry, Shakespeare again!) and, most importantly, you will be able to move forward in your life and fulfill your true potential.

So, let's get started!

PART 1: PREPARING FOR CONFIDENCE

In order to change, you need to understand what you are dealing with.
This section of the book will give you a background and a foundation to build on.

Chapter 1: Defining Terms

"Before anything else, preparation is the key to success."
Alexander Graham Bell

Two terms we will use quite a lot in this book are self-esteem and self-confidence. They are often used interchangeably, but actually there is an important difference. You can have high self-esteem and low self-confidence and vice versa.

Self-esteem, according to an article by Dr. Neel Burton in Psychology Today, is *"derived from the Latin aestimare, meaning to 'appraise, value, rate, weigh, estimate,' and our self-esteem is our cognitive and, above all, emotional appraisal of our own worth. More than that, it is the matrix through which we think, feel, and act, and reflects and determines our relation to ourselves, to others, and to the world."*

If you have a healthy level of self-esteem, then you value and respect yourself. You don't try to inflict damage on yourself through toxic relationships or alcohol and drug abuse. You don't need praise, a high salary, a big house, fancy car or an important-sounding job title to make yourself feel good. You are resilient and can bounce back after failure and even rejection, because you don't take them personally. One of your mantras may well be *"shit happens."*

If self-esteem is an internally-driven quality then self-confidence is more of an outward and worldly one. Derived from the Latin fidere – to trust, the self-confident person, according to Dr. Burton, has *"trust in oneself, and in particular, in one's ability or aptitude to engage successfully, or at least adequately, with the world."*

The Cambridge English dictionary puts it this way: **Self-confident (adj.): behaving calmly because you have no doubts about your ability or knowledge.**

Interesting they have mentioned "behaving calmly", isn't it? Maybe you haven't thought about self-confidence being linked to calmness before, but it does seem to be a key component. Test it out. Imagine you have to make a speech, or meet new people at a party, or present a report at a meeting. (Feel free to add your most scary scenario here.) How do you usually feel in this situation? Try and really get into it. Chances are you're experiencing wild and wayward butterflies, shaky hands, and a heart that is pounding so violently you are sure it is about to burst out from your chest like something from the film Alien. In case you need it spelled out further, this is the very opposite of calm. You don't need to be a rocket scientist to appreciate why a calm approach is a good thing. You think straight, you make good decisions, you deal effectively with situations and you inspire and reassure others. Calm is good.

The dictionary says you feel calm *"because you have no doubts about your ability or knowledge."* So, another crucial aspect of being self-confident is that you understand what abilities or knowledge you have, and have faith in them. It sounds very simple when you put it like that, doesn't it? But then simple doesn't always mean easy, or you would be flying through every slightly hair-raising situation with no qualms or quivers at all!

In the introduction, we mentioned an article that said low self-confidence could be a good thing, because it makes you work harder and not rest on your laurels. Therefore, another aspect of self-confidence that seems to be important is not to have too much of it. If not kept in check, confidence can turn to cockiness or arrogance, which are unattractive and unpopular traits.

However, in the right measure, self-confidence is an attractive quality. People feel relaxed around someone confident, rather than awkward or embarrassed in their company. Self-confidence allows you to maximize your potential and use your skills and talents to enrich your life and the lives of others. It means you are willing to experience all kinds of events and situations, even if they don't work out, rather than sit on the sidelines because you are too scared or self-conscious to try. A healthy level of self-confidence allows you to live effectively. It is not about getting the most out of life, but about getting the best out of life.

You can see how it is possible to have a high level of self-esteem and a low level of confidence, particularly when you consider that self-confidence is often linked to a specific area of life. Speaking personally, I have a healthy level of self-esteem but a very low level of self-confidence in cooking or freeway driving!

Self-confidence is often raised or eroded through feedback and experience. People who stretch themselves and step outside their comfort zones will build their self-confidence. I know if I cook several successful meals for friends, rather than cop out and take them to the pizzeria as I usually do, my self-confidence on the cooking front will improve.

And if you consider the opposite way around, examples of high self-confidence and low self-esteem are numerous. You have only got to look at the world of show-business to find talented and self-confident artists who think nothing of singing, dancing, telling jokes or acting in front of millions of people and yet end up dying from drug abuse, because deep down they don't value themselves.

Why Growing Confidence, Assertiveness & Self-Esteem Is So Essential

There are proven health benefits, both physical and mental, to having a good level of self-esteem and self-confidence. The Journal of Research in Personality published a fascinating paper in 2010 by psychologist Andy Martens of the University of Canterbury, Christchurch, New Zealand and his team.

They were investigating whether a good level of self-esteem could protect the immune system and heart. Their experiments involved giving a group of individuals fake feedback about themselves which would raise or lower their self-esteem. (Basically, if you tell someone they are stupid or brilliant enough times they are going to believe you, whether it is true or not.) They then analyzed whether or not this affected their physiology. Although the effect wasn't massive, it was statistically significant. They proved that people with higher levels of self-esteem had higher cardiac vagal tone, something which is linked to heart rate and is used as an indicator of stress. In other word, they proved that the higher the level of self-esteem, the lower the level of stress.

When looking at mental health, there have been many studies over the years showing a link between low self-esteem and psychiatric disorders. A 2003 report on low self-esteem and psychiatric patients by Peter Silverstone and colleagues from the Department of Psychiatry at the University of Alberta, Canada, concluded: *"the results of the present study demonstrate that all psychiatric patients suffer some degree of lowered self-esteem. Furthermore, the degree to which self-esteem was lowered differed amongst various diagnostic groups. Self-esteem was lowest in patients with major depressive disorders, eating disorders and substance abuse."*

That isn't to say that if you have low self-esteem you have a psychiatric problem – far from it – but it is easy to see why building a good level of self-esteem will have a positive impact on your mental health.

Where Are You Now?

Now we have got to grips with the terminology, the next thing to do is assess where you are now in terms of both self-esteem and self-confidence. So here is a self-assessment quiz so we can get the lie of the land, so to speak.

Self-Esteem Assessment

This is the Rosenberg Self-Esteem Scale, first developed in 1965. There are ten questions and four possible answers: strongly agree, agree, disagree or strongly disagree. Choose the first one that comes to mind, don't think too hard! For each question write down the number of your answer in brackets and then add up the score which will be between 0 and 30. Ready? Ok here we go!

On the whole, I am satisfied with myself: Strongly Agree (3), Agree (2), Disagree (1), Strongly Disagree (0)

At times, I think I am no good at all: Strongly Agree (0), Agree (1), Disagree (2), Strongly disagree (3)

I feel that I have a number of good qualities: Strongly Agree (3), Agree (2), Disagree (1), Strongly Disagree (0)

I am able to do things as well as most other people: Strongly Agree (3), Agree (2), Disagree (1), Strongly Disagree (0)

I feel I do not have much to be proud of: Strongly Agree (0), Agree (1), Disagree (2), Strongly disagree (3)

I certainly feel useless at times: Strongly Agree (0), Agree (1), Disagree (2), Strongly disagree (3)

I feel that I'm a person of worth, at least on an equal plane with others: Strongly Agree (3), Agree (2), Disagree (1), Strongly Disagree (0)

I wish I could have more respect for myself: Strongly Agree (0), Agree (1), Disagree (2), Strongly Disagree (3)

All in all, I am inclined to feel that I am a failure: Strongly Agree (0), Agree (1), Disagree (2), Strongly Disagree (3)

I take a positive attitude towards myself: Strongly Agree (3), Agree (2), Disagree (1), Strongly Disagree (0)

Now it is time to look at what your score means. Basically, the higher the score, the higher your self-esteem. If you score below 15, you are likely to have low self-esteem.

Self-Confidence Assessment

This test is in a different format to the one above because it is entirely subjective. This is because, as mentioned earlier, your self-confidence can vary depending on the role you are playing and the situation you are in.

Make a list of the different "hats" you wear in your life: for example, partner, sibling, teacher, friend, parent, farmer, organizer, cook, gardener, carer, child, negotiator, financial manager, nurse etc.

For Example: I am a writer (my job) but also wife, sister, friend, farmer (I keep animals, but am not a real farmer!), counselor (a lot of friends ask me for advice), financial manager (in the sense I have to manage my own accounts), weaver, cook, foreign language speaker … you get the idea. Make the list as long as it needs to be to cover the important things in your life.

For each role, write a few key things that you do which need a degree of confidence.

For Example: Cook: prepare meals for family, cook for friends, entertain guests formally (work)

Give each of those a score out of 10 for how confident you feel. The higher the score, the more confident you feel doing it. This is subjective, so you need to think about what the numerical scores mean to you. Example: cook: prepare meals for family – 7, cook for friends – 5, entertain guests formally (work) – 2.

Circle all the scores where you consider you have an acceptable or good score for confidence. (Again, this is subjective, you may consider 7 an acceptable score, someone else may think only 8 or above is acceptable. It doesn't matter, this is your test and only you are going to see it!)

Congratulate yourself on the fact you have demonstrated confidence in several key areas of your life. If you can do it in one area, then you can do it in others.

Now look at the areas where you feel you need more confidence. Maybe prioritize them, so you can focus on one or two areas and don't feel overwhelmed.

Important note: Even if you don't consider yourself a very self-confident person, there is always going to be something in life you feel confident about doing, so make sure you have included that in your list. OK, you may have rated yourself a 1 for giving presentations at work, but you may be a 10 for being a shoulder to cry on, or teaching your child to read, or training your dog. Don't neglect those. They are important!

Now that you have completed the two quizzes, you should have an idea of your current level of self-esteem and self-confidence. Don't judge yourself, that's not why we're doing this. You are where you are and that's fine for now. It's just important to have some kind of bench-mark at the start so that you can map your progress.

You might have been surprised at the fact self-esteem and self-confidence are different. You might also never have thought about the fact that you can have different levels of self-confidence in different areas of your life. Interesting, isn't it?

"Know yourself to improve yourself."
Auguste Comte

A Vital Skill To Learn

You may already write in a journal, but if not, it's a good idea to start, specifically for this project. Do not worry, nobody is going to see it except you, so write or draw whatever you like.

The thing about keeping a journal is to **keep doing it**. Even if it's just a few words a day, or one picture. Think of it like a caring friend you can tell anything to. Here are some suggestions to help you at the start:

- Think of an image, simile or metaphor to describe how you feel when thinking about self-confidence. (Example: When I think about self-confidence I feel like I am ploughing through a bog and could get sucked under at any moment.)
- Add your quiz results and your feelings about the results. Did anything surprise or fascinate you?
- Make a note of what you understand about the difference between self-confidence and self-esteem.
- List the things you are confident about.
- List one or two areas you would like to improve.
- Write 5 things in your life you are grateful for.
- Add inspirational quotations or pictures.
- Write the biographies of people you consider role models.
- Imagine you are now self-confident in the areas of life that are important to you. How does that feel? Write it down!

Singing for Self Esteem

In the late 1980s in the Brazilian city of Belo Horizonte, life for working class women was hard, particularly in the favelas – the slums.

Many of the women were of African descent and were on anti-depressants or sleeping pills to block out the pain of their daily existence. In the favela of Alto Vera Cruz, Community organizer Valdete da Silva Cordeiro noticed how most of the older black women went to the Health Center to get mind-numbing prescription medication. She realized that they needed to regain their self-esteem and to be given a way to focus on the positive aspects of lives that were depressing and filled with chores.

It was difficult at first to get the women to look at the small but positive things in life. She says: *"It was a big struggle to form this group. There were women who didn't even enjoy being here. They were always running around. When it was time to relax we would say, 'Now, lay back and relax, close your eyes, think about good things. Think about flowers, water ...'"*

She persevered and invited the women to have informal chats, which led to arts and craft sessions. Because they had never had a proper childhood, Valdete encouraged them to play games and sing songs which led to the formation of a singing group, the Meninas de Sinha.

Valdete is quoted as saying: *"From this day if you ask me how did we get to the point of performing all over the Brazil, including performing with such big stars such as Daniel Mercury and Jair Rodrigues, I would not know how to explain. We have been in governmental events, we have recorded CDs and even met the Culture Minister, Gilberto Gil. And if you ask me how did we manage this, I really*

21

would not know how to explain to you. All I know is that everything you do with love, grows."

Although Valdete has now died, the choir is still going strong. The women's ages range from 50 to 93. The simple truth of what she did obvious. She built on small, positive things and gave the women confidence. She encouraged them to treat themselves with compassion and helped rebuild their self-esteem. Small steps led to bigger ones as the women began to realize that they could do things they had never imagined themselves capable of.

You can do the same!

Dealing with the Ups and Downs

You're setting off on an exciting journey and it's going to be a lot of fun. But like all journeys, there will be setbacks and pitfalls along the way. You will sometimes feel like you're getting nowhere, treading water. You may even feel like giving up. Don't worry. This is completely normal. Nothing worthwhile in life is ever completely plain sailing. As long as you are aware that there will be rough patches and down days, but you are kind to yourself and just keep going anyway, then you will be fine.

Chapter 1: Key Take-Aways

In this chapter you have learned:

- Self-esteem is how much you value yourself.

- Self-confidence is how much trust you have in your abilities and knowledge in a specific area.

- Calmness is a crucial factor.

- You can have high self-esteem and low self-confidence and vice versa.

- Too much self-confidence or self-esteem is as bad, or worse, than too little. No-one likes a smart-ass!

- A healthy level of self-confidence and self-esteem has numerous benefits, including a positive effect on your physical and mental health.

- A healthy level of self-confidence and self-esteem benefits not only you, but also those around you.

- Self-confidence varies depending on the role you are playing and the area of life you are dealing with.

- You are already self-confident in some areas of life.

- Keeping a journal is a good idea.

- There will be times when things don't go so well. This is quite normal. Just accept it and keep going anyway.

It's all very well understanding an issue and making plans for how to deal with it. But you know that feeling when sometimes, even armed with a lot of information and good intentions, you just can't get started? You might even be saying to yourself that this all sounds pretty hard and it might be better to stay where you are, because at least it's familiar. There's a reason for that hesitation. It's called fear. And that's what we're going to look at next.

Chapter 2 - Dealing With Fear

"Courage is resistance to fear, mastery of fear – not absence of fear."
Mark Twain

When humans first walked the earth, everyday life was genuinely physically risky. People must have been scared the whole time. But back then, feeling scared actually had a valid function. Numerous threats, from wild animals to hostile tribe-members, meant that fear was a healthy, necessary and useful emotional reaction. This is because, in dangerous situations, the **flight-or-fight response** is triggered. The adrenal glands kick in, flooding the body with stress hormones like adrenalin, cortisol and norepinephrine, tensing muscles, increasing heart rate, raising blood pressure and increasing energy, allowing you to run faster or fight better. When a sabre-tooth tiger is sizing you up for lunch, this is a pretty good thing.

The fight-or-flight (or freeze) response may be an ancient one, but it's still useful today when someone is faced with real danger. We've all read stories where a mother finds superhuman strength to lift a car off her trapped child. We can imagine what it's like to run full-pelt from an armed robber or jump from the window of a building being consumed in flames.

The problem comes when we get fearful or stressed about something that is not a physical threat. In this 21st-century world, most of us don't have to worry about being snatched up by a raptor or crushed by a herd of mammoths. Instead we fret about being talked about on social media, having an assessment at work or the in-laws coming to stay.
The trouble is that our brain doesn't differentiate between a physical or non-physical threat. If we feel upset and fearful,

the adrenal glands *still* release stress chemicals, it's just that we can't then work them out of our system by running away or fighting so they stay swooshing around in a toxic mix. Apart from their effects on our mental state, chronic fearfulness and stress can cause long term physical health effects in the body, including heart and blood pressure problems and risk of stroke.

So now you know what's going on in your body when you're afraid, you can see how it might be a good idea to tackle your self-imposed fears and save the fight-or-flight chemical boost for days when you have some real- life monsters to tackle.

Quickly Overcoming The Language of Fear

In English, there are numerous words to describe different aspects of fear, including worry, anxiety, insecurity, stress and panic. It can be quite useful to look at the meanings of some of those words and to consider how much they are related to real or imagined situations and to past, present or future time.

Fear is the feeling of being scared by a specific real or imagined danger. The focus is usually short term – the present and immediate future. If it spirals out of control fear can lead to panic. An example of a real fear would be getting hit by a train if your car breaks down on a level crossing. An example of an imagined fear would be that there is someone hiding under your bed as you lie there in the dark. Whether real or imagined, with fear, you want to escape from the situation, or avoid it in the first place.

Anxiety and worry are not about specific and immediate threats but about imagining possibilities. Although we may use both words interchangeably, they *aren't* the same thing. To help us understand this, let's turn to an interesting article in *Psychology Today* by *Guy Winch: 10 Crucial Differences Between Worry and Anxiety.*

In this, he describes how their are different psychological states and we experience them differently. *"We tend to experience worry in our heads and anxiety in our bodies,"* he writes, adding later: *"worry is verbally focused while anxiety includes ... mental imagery."* Another interesting distinction is that *"worry often triggers problem solving, but anxiety does not."* Winch's article goes on to explain that while worry can be short-term, controllable and often caused by realistic concerns, anxiety can be longer-term, cause serious emotional distress and can even *"jump from one focus to another."*

We have just looked at some words and tried to define them, but did you know that there is a branch of psychology which studies whether we feel an emotion less strongly if we don't have a word to describe it? Isn't that an interesting thought? That the language you use may influence your feelings, rather than the other way around. That if you don't have a word for something, maybe you don't experience it. This tells us a lot about our own culture and the importance and significance we attach to language and to certain emotions. Here's an intriguing example.

The Moken people are a small nomadic group living on houseboats in an island area between Burma and Thailand. They rely on fishing to survive and are more at home in the sea than on land. They have a close relationship with nature and a strong oral tradition. That, in itself, is fascinating. What is even more interesting for our purposes is that their language has no word for *"worry"*. That doesn't mean that people don't feel afraid. There is almost certainly a word in their language for fear. But given their lifestyle and culture, they probably focus more on real and present dangers like being eaten by a shark or drowning than fretting over things that may or may not happen at some point in the future.

The point is that if worrying was a universal human emotion, like fear, then all cultures would have a word for it. The fact that some don't, implies that worry is learned behavior linked strongly to culture. And if we can learn to worry, then we can just as easily learn not to worry as well – right?

What Are You Doing?

Does it help to define what you are feeling? To know the difference between fear, worry and anxiety? If speaking in public gives you the heebie jeebies, does it really matter what you call it? I think it does.

Knowledge is power. Thinking deeply about something that is causing you problems and then pulling it apart so you understand what is going on is a part of starting to tackle and resolve it. Let's try this now. We're going to look at a self-confidence issue you have. Read these questions and start to do some deep thinking. Bring your problem into the daylight. When you are ready, write down your answers in your journal.

Choose one area of your life which concerns you and write it down. Be specific. As we said in chapter 1, you may be confident *"wearing one hat"* and yet have problems in another situation. Don't write: *"I lack self confidence in cooking"*. Drill down. Is it all cooking? To repeat the personal example from the first chapter, I am quite happy cooking a snack for myself, but have issues when providing dinner for people I don't know well. So, I could write: *"I lack self-confidence when cooking meals for strangers."*

When you think about doing the specific thing you have written about, how do you feel? Again, be specific. Don't just write: *"I'm petrified of cooking for strangers."* Better would be: *"The thought of cooking for strangers gives me a heavy feeling in the pit of my stomach and a dry throat. I also want to run away."*

How likely is it that you will have to do the thing you have written about? In my example, realistically, I have only got to cook for strangers once a year, if that!
In the worst-case scenario (in my case, messing up the dinner for my business guests,) could the thing you have written about be a real physical or emotional threat? Are you in actual danger?

Looking at your answers, would you say you are dealing with a fear or a worry? (In my case, cooking for strangers once a year is more accurately described as a worry about looking a fool at some undefined point in the future, than a fear for my life. Being afraid of being stung if your neighbor keeps bees in your garden and you are allergic is an understandable fear.)

This exercise does several useful things. It names the problem and looks at how likely it is to happen to you. It asks you to define how you feel. Butterflies, a dry mouth, pins and needles, a churning stomach and a light head are often linked to anxiety and worry than the sudden physical reaction you get if you are afraid, like if someone pulls a gun on you in the street. It establishes if it is a specific threat, in which case fear (and the fight-or-flight response it triggers) is a good and understandable reaction which could save your life, or an energy-draining worry about a non-life-threatening, imagined situation.

What Are You Saying?

As we have seen, words are important. Defining things helps pin down the problem. But words are important in another way too. I'm talking about the words we use to ourselves, whether they are spoken out loud or the voices in our heads.

Expressions used repeatedly have an impact, but you may not even be aware that you are doing it. Once you start noticing the language you use regularly, then it may surprise you. To start this process, simply become aware, without judgment, of what you are saying over a period of a day or so. Maybe you use expressions like: *"I'm such an idiot,"* or *"I'm so stupid,"* or *"I'm always screwing up."* You don't have to be Carl Jung to see the message you are sending yourself there.

 Some self-talk is less obvious, but no less harmful. For example: *"I'm afraid, I can't make the meeting,"* or *"I'm really worried about tonight,"* or *"The nightmare scenario is that we don't get the contract,"* or *"I'm so terrified that we miss the deadline."*

You need to understand that all of those emotional, fear-based words and expressions are are feeding your mind. By constantly using this kind of language, you are reinforcing the belief that there are many awful things out there in the big bad world and that you are scared of them.

If you discover, after a couple of days of observation, that you tend to favor certain negative words or expressions, then make a concerted effort to stop berating yourself. Try to rephrase in order to remove the personal fear association. Build in some more empowering thoughts. So *"I'm really worried about tonight,"* could instead be: *"Tonight might be a problem, but I'm sure I can handle it."* Or even, *"Tonight may turn out to be really good!"*

It is not easy to retrain yourself and you will likely stumble a lot over this, but it's worth doing. You are not a hostage to your thoughts. You **can** take back control. You **can** change. Be kind to yourself and take it gently. It doesn't matter if you find yourself using the same old negative self-talk out of habit, the important thing is you are now aware of how much you're doing it and you can take steps to combat it.

"You may not control all the events that happen to you, but you can decide not to be reduced by them."
Maya Angelou

A Huge Lie We Must Address

A common misconception about self-confident people is that they are not afraid of anything and breeze though situations that freak out those who are less confident. This sets the bar pretty high if you are trying to build your own self-confidence. Understandably, this is a daunting task and, because we humans tend to favor the familiar over the unfamiliar, even if it isn't doing us any good, you may decide it is all far too risky and you are better with the quivering little "devil you know".

But it is important to state that self-confidence isn't about losing all fear or banishing all worry. It is about feeling uncomfortable and doing something anyway. The fear or anxiety doesn't go away, you just accept it and move forward. That's a courageous approach. An approach that is also useful, because your brain learns that you have done this once and survived. Therefore, you can do it again.

Breaking Through the Fear

One of the most inspirational spiritual leaders of recent times, Mahatma Gandhi, led the movement for Indian independence from British rule in the first half of the 20th century, using non-violent means. This unassuming-looking little man with his round glasses and dressed in a simple Indian dhoti was a trained lawyer who qualified in London, England. He went on to speak up for those who could not speak up for themselves, through numerous campaigns, rallies, speeches and media appearances.

Yet Gandhi was terrified by what he described as *"the awful strain of public speaking"*. As a law student, he had to give a speech at London's Vegetarian Society, but could only make it through the first line. *"My vision became blurred and I trembled,"* is how he described the paralyzing fear. He had to hand it to someone else to read for him.

In 1889, during his first case as a young lawyer he froze during cross examination and ran out of the courtroom. *"My head was reeling and I felt as though the whole court was doing likewise. I could think of no questions to ask,"* he said, recalling the humiliation of the moment.

It was only when he went to South Africa as a legal adviser that he started speaking in public. He didn't suddenly lose his nerves. He simply found that the reason for having to speak - to campaign against the racism and prejudice shown to Indians under British rule – was stronger than the fear. If he wanted to protest against something, if he wanted to bring to the public's attention something he was passionate about, he had to speak in public. It was as simple as that.

Gandhi always gave his speeches and interviews in a quiet, and at times hesitant, voice. But he used what could have been viewed as a handicap as an advantage. This is what he said, and it is an excellent example of reframing: *"My hesitancy in speech, which was once an annoyance, is now a pleasure. Its greatest benefit has been that it has taught me the economy of words."*

Some Strategies To Quickly & Easily Tackle Fear and Worry

There are a number of techniques you can use to tackle fear and worry. Owning the feeling and not berating yourself for it is a good start. Everyone is afraid or worried about something, after all. Here are a few different ideas to try. Read them through and try out those that appeal to you. Then try out those that don't because often things we shy away from are the most powerful.

- How about reframing fear as "excitement" or "anticipation." How would that feel? If instead of saying "I'm terrified of making presentations at work," you instead said: "I'm excited about making presentations at work."

- Stop watching or reading the news. Fear and general anxiety is often fueled by the media and 24/7 rolling news. Yes, some people say, "I'm a media junkie," or "I really need to know what's going on in the world." Really? If it's important enough, you'll find out. The problem with our

21st-century media is that it needs to find dramatic stories all the time to fill air-time. Dramatic usually means focusing on the worst aspects of things in a visual format, which is one of the best ways to convey "information" to we humans. Events that are statistically highly unlikely to happen to us suddenly fill our living rooms and make us believe we are in imminent danger. Watching gory and horrific images of suffering over and over and over again has a brainwashing effect. Little wonder we feel waves of unfocussed anxiety as we go about our daily lives.

- Don't saw sawdust. In other words, once an event is in the past, leave it there. If you can do something about a situation, then by all means do it. But if you are just spending hours chewing over what you could have said or done about something that is now over, it is wasted energy.

- Sit up straight! You were probably told that as a child, weren't you? Turns out there is a lot of truth in this. Changing the position of your body has a marked effect on your mind. Social psychologist Amy Cuddy has researched how certain expanded positions – what she calls "power poses" - affect confidence. She revealed her findings in 2012 in one of the most popular TED talks ever, **Your Body Language Shapes Who You Are**. Although some of her findings related to the physiological effects of power posing have been criticized, there is little doubt that expanded poses make people feel more confident.

- Breathe. Consciously breathing deeply and steadily has a calming effect and has been proven to lower blood pressure and reverse the effects of "fight-or-flight."

- Read some statistics. They can reassure you or even make you laugh. For example, your chances of dying by being hit by debris falling from outer space is one in 100 billion, in case you were worried about that!

Chapter 2: Key Take-Aways

In this chapter, we have looked at:

- The fight-or-flight response to fear and how it is a useful reaction when you are genuinely in danger.

- The difference between fear (real or imagined), anxiety and worry.

- The importance of identifying the emotion you are feeling and assessing if you are in genuine danger.

- The power of language. How self-talk can be negative but can be turned into a positive by reframing.

- The need to act courageously. Even if you are fearful or worried, go ahead and do it anyway.

- Some strategies to deal with fear and worry.

Chapter 3 – Overcoming Fear To Build Self-Esteem and Confidence

As we saw from the example of Gandhi, fear can be overcome if you have a powerful enough motivation to do it. What fires you up? What are you passionate about? It can help you move mountains. That's what we're going to talk about in this chapter.

"It is good to love many things, for therein lies the true strength, and whosoever loves much performs much, and can accomplish much, and what is done in love is well done."
Vincent Van Gogh

There is a common misconception, reinforced by the popular adage: *"Do what you love and the money will follow,"* that everyone has a single mysterious passion that needs to be uncovered and once it sees the light of day, your life will be filled with rainbows and unicorns. As a result of this revelation, you will change jobs and make a ton of money. This is all very well for those lucky people who have a single passion that they can home in on (and cash in on) with laser focus. Good for them! But it can leave the rest of us thinking that we are hopeless, inadequate individuals because either we can't find "The Thing," or we find it, but don't necessarily want to make money from it.

You don't need to waste time looking for the one passion, the self-help Holy Grail, because it doesn't exist. Here's the truth. Ready? Most people love more than one thing. They don't have a passion, but passions. Some big, some small, some they could make money from and some not. And it's all cool and it's all allowed. Shocker.

That isn't to say that passions are unimportant. Quite the reverse. Discovering what you love, and therefore what motivates you, is an important part of building your self-esteem and self-confidence. Once you are aware of the things that make you tingle with excitement, you can use the inspiration and focus you get from them in all kinds of situations from the mundane to the terrifying.

Love is a great motivator. Not just the love you feel for a person or animal, but love for an idea, a cause, a subject or the work you do. Love can overcome fear, self-consciousness, procrastination and lack of confidence. It can move mountains and accomplish miracles.

So, what do you love? Do you know? Many people haven't really given this too much thought, but it's something that needs to be studied and acted on. The simple act of identifying your passions can have surprising and profound results in all areas of your life, including those we are working on in this book.

Discovering New Strengths and Talents

"Passion is energy. Feel the power that comes from focusing on what excites you."
Oprah Winfrey

There are enough books, websites, blogs, YouTube channels and Facebook pages devoted to this topic to keep you busy for the rest of your life. Google is your friend, so enter some key phrases and enjoy! To avoid the danger of becoming addicted to discovering what you are passionate about, here are a few ideas to start with, that you may not have seen before:

Home Inventory: There are clues all around you, so do some treasure hunting in your own home. Look at your books, pictures, ornaments, DVDs, your rooms and your yard. What would a stranger make of what they see? How would they sum you up from what you have chosen to surround yourself with? (You could even ask a friend to do this for you.) Now, what do you make of your choices? The answers may surprise you.

I remember someone visiting my home for the first time saying to me: *"You really love birds, don't you?"* Upon seeing my confused expression she pointed out all my bird-related stuff (and there was a lot). But I had honestly never noticed this before! Although I love birds, further thought revealed that my subconscious was asking me to focus on the freedom birds represent, rather than telling me to buy a pet parrot or start an albino peacock-breeding business in the back yard.

Imaginary Magazine Subscription: Go to a website like Amazon.com and browse magazine subscriptions. Imagine someone has gifted you subscriptions to five magazines (or ten if you like) for a year. Go ahead and make your choice. Don't overthink this, enjoy it. (Remember: don't really subscribe, this is just a game. And "buying things with credit cards" does not count as a justifiable passion – just saying!) Once you have your list, look at your choices and see what they tell you about your passions and true interests. Any link to what you discovered in the home inventory?

Journal Analysis: This only works if you have kept a journal for some time. If you haven't, no problem, skip this. If you have, then go through your journal for the past few months with a highlighter pen. Mark all the times where you wrote that you were happy, absorbed or enjoying yourself. What were you doing at the time to make you feel that way? Write a list. Now see if these link with the magazine subscriptions and inventory. They may not, it doesn't matter.

Revisit the Past: It is a cliché to say that what you loved doing as a child is revealing, but clichés usually contain a nugget of truth. As well as mining your own memories, take the excuse to visit with relatives or friends who knew you when you were young and ask them what they remember about you back then. What were you crazy about? What did you spend hours doing? Add these to your list of passions.

Your Perfect Day/Your Day from Hell: Take some quiet time out and relax. Imagine you could put together a perfect day, the kind of day you will rhapsodize about when you are 100 years old and looking back on your life. Go through it in detail from the moment you wake up to the moment you go to bed. Describe it in detail either by using a voice recorder or writing it down. Where are you? Who are you with? How do you spend these magical 24 hours?

As before, think about your answers and see what they tell you about your passions. If you find this hard, or want to try just for fun, reverse the process and describe a day from hell. The idea with this is that you look at the description like a photo negative. Analyze what you have written and then reverse it, and you will have a clue as to what you really love!

By this time, you should have a reasonable list of things that fire you up. Some may be creative, some may not, some might be huge and some small. The point is, these things stir your soul and inspire you and they belong to you alone. You now need to make sure you act on them.

Spend time doing even **one** small thing that thrills you. Feel how amazing that is. Make a conscious decision to include more of the things on your list in your life and then start doing it.

Passion and Self-Confidence

"You either walk inside your story and own it or you stand outside your story and hustle for your worthiness."
Brene Brown

Understanding and acting on what you love can really help you build self-confidence and self-esteem. Here's how:

- The very act of looking for your passions and doing the exercises above (or other ones) increases your self-esteem. It is good for you to dig deep. It tells your subconscious that its messages are being listened to and taken seriously.

- Time spent thinking about things that make you feel good encourages your brain to build new neural pathways and "get into the habit" of being positive.

- The list of passions underscores your uniqueness. There is no-one on earth quite like you, with your combination of experience, passions, talents and skills.

- Making time for something you love doing, even if it is only a short time doing a small thing, encourages you to follow your authentic self.

- Doing something new or that scares you every day is a good thing to do, everyone tells you that. When the thing you are doing is something you love, then it is a lot less scary and a lot more motivating.

- It teaches you to "fail safely". For example, you may love painting, but your first attempt at a portrait may look more like your Setter than your sitter. Even if your pictures of people look more like your pets, it doesn't matter. It teaches you, in a safe way, that you can fail and the world doesn't end. Failure is just another outcome. You need to keep trying in order to progress.

Really Knowing Yourself

People have understood the importance of self-knowledge for thousands of years. The phrase "know thyself" is inscribed in stone at the Temple of Apollo at Delphi, in Greece, although it is thought to have originated in Ancient Egypt. The Greek philosopher Plato used it a lot in his famous dialogues with Socrates.
That's not to say that knowing what makes you tick is an easy task. One of the Founding Fathers of the United States Benjamin Franklin wrote in 1750: *"There are three things extremely hard: steel, a diamond and to know one's self."*

Don't let that put you off. Nothing worthwhile is ever achieved without some degree of effort. And it's not something that you cannot achieve in a day or a week, no matter how many quizzes and questionnaires you fill in! Getting to know yourself is a life-long task, but an essential and fruitful one. It means you are operating from a stable core of values. It means that you acknowledge your strengths and that you also recognize and accept your weaknesses. That you know what interests, motivates and excites you and look for ways to include more of those things in your life. Being who you truly are, sets you free.

Accepting who you are means being kind to yourself, "warts and all" (unless you have the inclination to pull the legs off spiders, kittens or people, in which case you need more help than this book can give you. Get some professional advice - now!) Your temperament may incline more towards introvert than extrovert. That is totally fine, it's who you are. Extroverts are not better or worse than introverts, they are just different. So be kind to yourself. Don't try to change your basic personality, interests or preferences to please others.

Discovering & Growing Your Inner Superhero

"Calm mind brings inner strength and self-confidence, so that's very important for good health."
Dalai Lama

One of the best things you can do as you begin your journey of self-discovery is to meet your Inner Superhero. This is the part of you that always has your best interests at heart and will fight tooth and nail to protect you from bad guys like Self Sabotage and your Inner Critic. You know, those little voices in your head that tells you're not good/clever/tall/thin/outgoing/confident enough? The ones that look at a great opportunity or relationship and insist that you don't deserve it so why not mess it up first, before someone else does? Yes, I thought you might recognize those two. They are doing you no good at all. Luckily, you have a way of foiling their plans.

Your Inner Superhero can take any form you want. In fact, it can be quite fun to set aside some time and go meet them.

Find a quiet spot and relax. Close your eyes and then create in your imagination a special sanctuary, a place you can feel safe. It can look be anywhere you wish – up a mountain, in a forest, by the ocean, in a penthouse, even in the sky - and be furnished in whatever way makes you happy. You can return to this place whenever you want as often as you want and you will always feel calm, safe and protected.

Once you have created this sanctuary, summon your Inner Superhero and see what happens. If you are good at visualization then a very vivid image may come to mind. Not everyone can visualize easily and that's fine, just get a sense of their positive and loving presence. If you can't sense anything then just imagine they are there, because they are.

You can spend some time getting to know your Inner Superhero and when you are ready, give them their instructions. That you want them to protect you from the Inner Critic and Self Sabotage and to alert you anytime those guys are around.

Outside Help
It's good to know that your Inner Superhero is always there to stand up for you and bring you courage and strength. But sometimes, if you feel that everything is up to you, that you are tackling life alone, it can be overwhelming. In this situation, it's immensely comforting to think that you are part of something bigger and that you can access some kind of higher power or energy.

Your own religious or spiritual beliefs can be very uplifting and reassuring. The knowledge that you are unconditionally loved and that you can offload problems, fears and worries to God or the Universe, or another positive beneficial force is an immensely positive thing.

What if you don't believe in anything or you're not sure? That's fine. This book is not trying to convert you or impose anything on you that you are not comfortable with. But if you are curious, if you would like to feel that you are in control of life events rather than have them control you, then you might consider exploring spiritual disciplines that don't necessarily involve any belief systems, such as yoga or meditation. We'll talk more about this in later chapters.

Heavenly Workforce

This is a very interesting technique to use for many different situations. It's adapted from a book called Hiring the Heavens by Jean Slatter. Basically, it involves "employing" a heavenly team of helpers, each an expert in a particular field, whom you ask to perform specific tasks for you. This "work for hire" group can be made up of anyone you wish, real or fictional, from the past, present or even the future. So, for example, you could hire Sherlock Holmes to track down your missing cat, or William Shakespeare to help you write a poem.

Suzi Wilson has been a big fan of using a heavenly workforce for a couple of years, since first discovering the technique. She'd been through a difficult divorce and although she was open to the idea of a new romantic relationship, it had been 20 years since she had last dated and she had lost a lot of confidence. *"I was terrified of making a fool of myself,"* she admits, *"and was convinced that no-one would find me in the least attractive, after all, I wasn't 21 anymore. And where would I meet anyone? Should I go on a dating website? Join a club? I had no clue. And zero confidence. I longed to be able to talk to my Mom, she always gave me great advice, but she passed ten years ago. My grandma was also great at boosting me up and telling me I could do things, but she had been dead for 25 years. And I also remember reading a novel when I was about 18, I can't remember who it was by, but the heroine was called Dora and she was feisty and funny and acted as a great matchmaker for all her friends. I would love to have got some words of wisdom from her."*

Suzi learned about hiring a heavenly workforce from one of her friends and decided to try. *"It seemed harmless – in fact it looked quite a lot of fun,"* she says, *"and so I thought I would hire a Romance Team!"* She explains that her imaginary team was made up of her mom, her grandma, Dora from the book and also the Greek goddess of love, Aphrodite. *"I added her because I thought I could do with the top expert,"* explains Suzi with a laugh.

Suzi started by having a meeting with her four consultants and giving them their orders. *"I visualized this great meeting room and us all sitting round a big table, with me running the meeting as I was the one doing the hiring. I handed out their roles. I put my grandma in charge of building my confidence. Dora from the book was to find me a few great people to date. My mom was in charge of selecting the right one and Aphrodite's job was to make the right one fall in love with me!"*

She goes on to explain that she had meetings every morning with her team and then *"I just let them get on with it. I didn't worry about how it was going to happen, I just gave them their jobs and trusted they would do a good job. I did follow any advice they gave me, like my grandma told me to go horseback riding again, something I used to be passionate about when I was in my early twenties, so I did that."*

To her great surprise, one year after hiring her Romance

Team, Dora is engaged to a great guy, James, who runs the local riding school, and is planning her wedding. *"Don't ask me how this has happened,"* she laughs. *"I can't quite believe it myself. All I know is that once I stopped worrying and handed everything over to my heavenly helpers, my romantic life took off! At one point I had three men who wanted to date me! Three! Luckily my mom helped narrow this down to the right one."*

You may not have results quite as spectacular as Dora, but you never know where hiring a heavenly team could take you…

Chapter 3: Key Take-Aways

In this chapter, we have looked at:

- How most people have more than one passion and the importance of finding yours.

- Different techniques to find out what you really love, including doing a home inventory and imagining a perfect day.

- How discovering and acting on your passions and interests can build self confidence.

- The importance of action and how you should take some steps, even small ones, towards

- Doing the things that motivate you.

- The phrase *'know thyself'* and the value of learning about and accepting who you are.

- How to access your own Inner Superhero to defeat the

twin baddies: Self Sabotage and the Inner Critic.

- The importance of help from a source of higher power outside yourself or of practicing some type of spiritual discipline.

- Getting help from your own heavenly workforce.

Part of knowing yourself is understanding your amazing brain and its abilities. Weighing little more than three pounds, about the size of a grapefruit and resembling the halves of a wrinkly gray walnut, the brain is so much more than a super computer running your mind and body. The next chapter reveals all.

Chapter 4 - Your Amazing Mind & What It Can Achieve

"You have power over your mind, not outside events. Realize this, and you will find strength."
Marcus Aurelius

This chapter is going to look at your own personal powerhouse, something that can literally change everything for you, the one thing you must understand and use properly in order to build self-confidence and achieve what you hope to in life. Of course, I am talking about your mind. It's something that very few of us know much about. There aren't *"how to master your mind"* lessons in most schools, even though it's one of the most influential and important factors in anyone's development.

Many people use the terms "mind" and "brain" interchangeably, but they are different, although exactly what that difference is has been controversial in the past. For hundreds of years, scientists and philosophers have argued over the correct definition of "the human mind" and "the human brain." In the last few decades, there have been big advances in neuroscience and brain imagery. This has allowed scientists to literally see the brain at work, giving them more information about different areas of the brain and what they are responsible for. Although there are still several points where people have different opinions, they seem to agree on the following:

- The mind is located in the brain

- "the mind is the brain at work" (Dr Joe Dispenza, Science and Consciousness Magazine)

- The brain needs to be alive for the mind to work

- The brain and body can be changed by thinking differently. (Research has shown that the brain doesn't differentiate between really doing an activity and imagining doing it.)

Let's look at the brain and mind in turn because it's vital to understand such crucial (and utterly incredible) parts of you.

Directing Your Brain To Achieve All You Want

The brain is pretty cool! This gray and white jelly-like wrinkly organ is divided into two hemispheres and is connected to the spinal cord via the brain stem. It is the center of the human nervous system, weighs about three pounds, has 100,000 miles of blood vessels and makes up about two percent of your total body weight. Its various parts control everything from the most basic functions like breathing and blood circulation, to the most complex ones like thinking and problem solving. The brain "runs" the body, via a network of nerves – 100 billion microscopic cells known as neurons which communicate with each other via trillions of synapses. You are born with most of the neurons you will ever have but many are not connected to each other. Performing new tasks and forming memories creates new connections (synapses) which are reinforced by repetition. This mostly happens during childhood. Scientists believe that as an adult, your brain can make some new neurons in the hippocampus, the brain region involved with learning and memory, and that new synapses can develop too.

The Mind

There are different definitions of the mind, according to which field of science you are in. But to simplify things, let us look at what Collins English dictionary says.

"mind
1. the human faculty to which are ascribed thought, feeling, etc. often regarded as the immaterial part of a person.
2.intelligence or the intellect esp. as opposed to feelings or wishes.
3. Recollection or remembrance; memory: it comes to mind
4. the faculty of original or creative thought; imagination: it's all in the mind..."

There's a lot more to the definition. In fact, if you look at the page, you can see it is one of the longest entries in the dictionary, which gives you a good indication of how complex the subject is!

A few years ago, the Dalai Lama gave a talk about the Buddhist concept of mind at a Mind Science Symposium at MIT in Cambridge, MA, USA. He made some interesting points: *"We can see from our experience that our state of mind plays a major role in our day-to-day experience and physical and mental well-being. If a person has a calm and stable mind, this influences his or her attitude and behavior in relation to others ... our mental attitude is a critical factor in determining our experience of joy and happiness, and thus our good health."*

He goes on say that the mind has many levels. There is the *"clear, light mind"* which has *"knowing, luminosity and clarity"* that spiritual seekers strive for, down to the grosser levels of mental consciousness *"such as our sensory perceptions, which cannot function or even come into being without depending on physical organs like our senses."*

The talk is very interesting and I'd encourage you to read it if you want to delve deeper into this subject. Let's pull out just one more nugget from what he said: *"Another distinctive feature of mind is that it has the capacity to observe itself. The issue of mind's ability to observe and examine itself has long been an important philosophical question. In general, there are different ways in which mind can observe itself. For instance, in the case of examining a past experience, such as things that happened yesterday you recall that experience and examine your memory of it...But we also have experiences during which the observing mind becomes aware of itself while still engaged in its observed experience."*

Apart from the incredible fact that the mind is capable of observing itself, we also have to understand that it operates on a conscious, subconscious and unconscious level. It can be helpful to think of this of these as three layers, each deeper than the one before.

The conscious mind is the top layer. It is what you are aware of at this moment. For example, you are aware that you are reading these words, that you are breathing as you read, that a bird is singing outside. You can also use your conscious mind to imagine something right now that isn't real, like a blue and pink elephant. The conscious mind probably accounts for about 10 percent of your brain's capability.

The subconscious mind is below the conscious mind. It is the part of consciousness that stores recent memories you need to access quickly. It is the filing cabinet for day-to-day stuff, like pin numbers, the names of new acquaintances, how to get from A to B. When your subconscious is at play, it is not in your awareness. But the information can be accessed once you think about it. If you have ever arrived at work and have absolutely no recollection of the trip there, then your subconscious mind has been at work, negotiating the familiar route and making sure you got there safely. You can easily bring this route to mind by thinking about it, even if you can't remember the exact journey! The subconscious mind probably accounts for about 50 – 60 percent of your brain's capabilities.

The unconscious mind, which takes up the remaining 30 - 40 percent, is like the bottom of the sea, or a better way of putting it might be a library at the bottom of the sea. It is the deepest layer and is pretty much inaccessible to our conscious minds. It contains buried memories and past experiences, those parts of you which shape your beliefs, habits and behaviors.

What if Thoughts are Things?

You may have read or heard about the idea that we can create our own reality with our minds. It sounds far-fetched. If true, it certainly brings into sharp focus the responsibility we carry in owning our thoughts and making sure we don't fill our minds with negativity.

Could it be true that consciousness creates reality? That the universe only comes into existence because we focus on it? Science does not exclude this possibility, in fact it is one of the big conundrums in physics.

Everything in the universe is made of energy. In terms of physics, things that appear solid (tables, tigers, trombones…) are made up of atoms which are mostly empty space. Matter has the illusion of solidity because of the way the atoms are bonded together. But if you trip over a Chihuahua and fall onto the sidewalk you know that this is more than mere illusion. In our day to day lives matter is solid and that it hurts!

Quantum physics has demonstrated that on sub-atomic level, the electrons and protons making up atoms aren't solid either. What's more, these tiny things can sometimes behave like particles and sometimes like waves. In itself, that is strange. Even stranger is that experiments show that these sub-atomic little guys are in a state of "potential" and the act of observation releases that potential. (If you are interested in learning more about wave/particle duality affected by observation then have a look at the famous "double slit" experiment.) Is your mind blown yet?

So, where does this information take us, in our quest to improve self-esteem and self-confidence? If science allows the possibility that conscious thought can affect the real world we live in, then it means that what goes on in our minds has a real effect. If you are constantly listening to that little voice in your head saying you are stupid, could never talk in public, or are a fraud that people will soon unmask then it will become a self-fulfilling prophecy, negativity building on negativity.

How to make sure your inner dialogue is a healthy and positive one

We have seen already that the mind does not distinguish between real and vividly imagined events and can build new neural pathways in either case. Therefore, it makes sense to use the power of your imagination to create strong, positive messages.

- Squash the critic! Become your own cheerleader and motivational coach.
- Replace "I can't" with "I can."
- Become aware of the present moment, it's all you have!
- Consciously celebrate any achievements, however small.

Growing Your Life To Great Prosperity

British empowerment and confidence coach and motivational speaker Sue Stone has been called the United Kingdom's happiest and most positive person. She has the home of her dreams in the countryside, a successful international media career and was recently featured in the Channel 4 TV show Secret Millionaire and How'd You Get So Rich? But her life wasn't always like this.

Back in 1999, Sue had three young children, over a quarter of a million dollars of debt, her marriage had broken down and she was facing the threat of her family home being repossessed. She had just $12 in her purse. Things couldn't have been worse and she knew she had to do something. That "something" was to learn everything possible about the subconscious mind and the power of thought. She read everything she could lay her hands on, researched the topic and decided to act on what she had learned. It didn't happen overnight, but gradually Sue's life improved

The single most important principle Sue says she discovered, and the one she lives her life by is this: you get more of what you focus on. Think about that for a second and you will see how it makes perfect sense. Focus on feelings of inadequacy, fear and lack and that is what you will see manifest in your life. Focus on happiness, fulfillment and confidence and that is what will show up instead. Which would you rather have?

The Great Hidden Skill That Changes Everything

We have already learned that the brain doesn't recognize the difference between a real experience and an imagined one. A study published in the Journal of Neurophysiology in 2014 illustrates this very nicely. Scientists at Ohio University in the USA took two groups of healthy people and immobilized one of their wrists by putting them in casts for four weeks. One group did nothing while those in the other group were told to sit still for 11 minutes and perform *"mental imagery of strong muscle contractions five days a week."* The experiment lasted for four weeks. Once the four-week period was up, scientists performed a series of tests on various aspects of flexibility and muscle strength of the affected wrist. They found that the group who had done the mental exercises were twice as strong as the control group. In addition, these participants' brains were also different. They had stronger neuromuscular pathways than those who did nothing.

Athletes too have long known that using visualization is a power aid to performance. Veteran tennis star Billie Jean King was among the first top names to use visualization in the 1960s. Decades later, there are now sports psychologists who train top sportsmen and women to employ the power of their minds. They encourage them to imagine and experience all aspects of a successful performance from going around the course in their mind's eye to getting presented with the trophy and speaking at the winner's press conference. In a fascinating article: Olympians Use Imagery as Mental Training in The New

York Times just before the 2014 Winter Olympics, writer Christopher Clarey quotes American aerialist Emily Cook who is explaining why she prefers the term "imagery". As what they are doing is a "multisensory endeavor", Cook says: *"Visualization for me, doesn't take in all the senses. You have to smell it. You have to hear it. You have to feel it, everything."*

If scientists have proved that the brain responds to imaginary exercise and top Olympians regularly incorporate "mind work" into their training, it is obvious that anyone who uses imagery to improve self-confidence is going to experience positive results. There will be more about this later in the book, but for now, we will follow the example of Emily Cook and employ all the senses possible when imagining a situation.

Try This!

Bring to mind a situation where you have felt less than confident. Try to imagine it in as much detail as possible.

- Are you inside or outside?
- What is the temperature?
- What are you wearing?
- Where are you standing?
- What can you see and smell and feel around you?
- What are you doing that needs confidence? (making a presentation? a speech? asking for a rise?)

Now imagine doing this thing that needs confidence. You feel amazing, you are the most relaxed and self-confident person in the world (without being cocky). How do confident people stand? Well, stand like that. How do they speak? Speak like that. Go through the whole thing in your mind as super confident you. Use as many senses as you can to see, feel, hear and smell the situation. Hear that applause, feel the pats on the back! Now how does that make you feel?

Remember, if you can do it in your mind, you can do it in real life.

Beating Procrastination

This is not easy and anyone who says it is a matter of willpower and just getting on with it is lying! If you have ever, during "work" hours, got sucked down the rabbit hole of checking your emails every two minutes, Googling how to measure the hottest chili pepper in the world, looking at all the Facebook photos of your high school crush or trying on all your outfits to see which ones go with your new sparkly shoes, then you know how bad it makes you feel. The instant gratification of avoiding what you should be doing does not compare to the satisfying feeling of achieving something you had to do, something that perhaps was quite hard and not that much fun.

We have seen that the brain responds to habitual activities by forging neural pathways. If we do something we have never tried, like learning to play the piano, then it is even capable of creating new neural pathways to accommodate this new habit. The problem is that the brain will also do the same for bad habits. It doesn't really discriminate. If you constantly procrastinate, never start projects on time, meet deadlines late, end up rushing around doing things at the last minute, then your mind will learn that this is your habitual behavior. In other words, you have successfully trained your mind, just like a top athlete, to respond in the same way to a challenge, whether it is writing a report, a book, starting exercise or learning a new language. *"I can't do this. It's too hard. I always fail at this stuff anyway. It's boring. It's not worth the effort. It's much more fun to do what I always do and watch some talking animals on YouTube."* And so the story goes on.

You need to create a new pattern that your mind can latch on to. A pattern that says you do complete projects, that you can stick with boring stuff, that your default position is not procrastination but action. Yes, you need to do stuff. Procrastinators hate doing stuff. They would much rather think about doing stuff or plan stuff to do. But the actual doing… oh well, that is quite a different story.

One good way to tackle this is to decide what is really important in your life. Something you would feel proud of achieving. For example, writing a novel or making a speech or travelling to Italy. Now break this huge task into small and specific bite-size chunks with specific deadlines. Write these chunks down. Now, take action! You need only spend ten minutes a day if that is all you think you can do consistently, but at least by the end of the week you will have spent 70 minutes on something important to you, rather than 70 minutes watching kittens being cute on YouTube.

Procrastination is a tricky enemy that is always lurking, ready to lure you down rabbit holes and away from worthwhile things by seductively offering brain-dead but fun alternatives. You only have one life. At the end of it do you want to say *"Well, that was a good life, I watched every episode of Friends three hundred times and know all there is to know about talking animals on YouTube."* Or do you want to say: *"I did everything I dreamed of doing. It was hard, at times it was boring, but at least I wrote my novel/saw Japan/learned to play the violin…"*
Your call.

Chapter 4: Key Take-Aways

In this chapter, we have looked at:

- The difference between the mind and the brain and how it is still controversial.

- Your conscious, subconscious and unconscious mind and how much of each you use.

- The possibility that "thoughts are things" and that the physical world can actually be influenced by your mind.

- How to ensure your inner dialogue is positive.

- How one woman turned her life around by using the power of positive thought and how you get what you focus on, so best make sure it is good!

- Scientific proof that a mental workout can have a physical effect.

- The power of visualization and why top athletes now call it imagery.

We have looked at the foundations for confidence building and how powerful your own resources are, so in Part Two we will be getting practical, giving you some techniques and tactics to try which will bring you closer to your goal of healthy self-confidence. We'll begin with something we've touched on in this chapter. Visualization and Imagery. Ready?

PART 2: STRATEGIES FOR SUCCESS

This section of the book uses the knowledge from Part One as a foundation for different techniques to build confidence.

Chapter 5 – Lets Create More Success Through Confidence, Assertiveness and Self-Esteem

"Imagination is the beginning of creation. You imagine what you desire, you will what you imagine and at last you create what you will."
George Bernard Shaw

In the last chapter, we learned that top athletes regularly use their imaginations to help them prepare for sporting events. Whether it's golfers going around an 18-hole course in their mind's eye or bob-sleighers visualizing every twist and turn of an icy track, the results are remarkable. Researchers have shown that the brain doesn't differentiate between a real event and a vividly imaged one. That's why people whose wrists were put in a plaster cast for a month but imagined flexing their muscles for a few minutes a day were shown to have less atrophy than those who did nothing.

Sports psychologists have used the technique for years, but if you remember, they encourage athletes to use all their senses to fully immerse themselves in the experience they are imagining. For this reason, they prefer to use the term "imaging" rather than "visualizing."
Musicians do it too, practicing scales or performing a piece of music in their minds to improve their performance. Famous concert pianist Arthur Rubenstein describes in his autobiography learning the piece Nights in the Gardens of

Spain by reading the score on train journeys and imagining playing it. Apparently, he played the whole thing from memory at the first rehearsal!

Some people find it easier to access their imagination than others, so what if you find it difficult to do this? Does it matter? I would encourage you to try. Practice as often as you can, because this is a technique that really does improve the more you use it. Even if you are not a "visual" person, you may be good at imagining a smell or sound or taste or feeling, and all of those things are very important. Obviously, the more complete and intense an experience the more effective it will be. Here are some tips to help you create an experience in your mind:

- Decide in advance exactly what you are going to imagine. If it is giving a successful speech for example, don't just pick any old situation. Be very specific.

- What is the subject? What time of year is it? How are you dressed and where will you be speaking? Is it early or late? How big is the audience? Are they old or young or a mixture?

- Are you on a stage or at a table? Is the room big or small? Do you have slides, video or nothing?

- Do you have notes or have you memorized your speech? How long are you going to speak for?

Once you have thought about the detail, or even written it down, then get in a comfortable position (lie down or sit in a comfortable chair). Close your eyes and calm yourself. This can be through breathing slowly and regularly, or focusing on relaxing your body starting at your toes and working up to your face and head. You might even like to use some relaxing music.

Now, using the power of your mind, imagine the scene you planned earlier. Using the speech example, see the room, hear the buzz of anticipation in the audience, look at what is in front of you and what is on the walls and the view from the window. Smell the room, feel the speech in your hands and the chair you are sitting on. Take a sip of water in your mind's eye and taste it as you swallow. Listen as you are introduced. Listen to that applause! They can't wait to hear you! Get to your feet and look confidently around the room. Smile and then start your speech. Look at how fascinated and entertained everyone is. They just love you and what you have to say. Finish to a standing ovation and then meet the crowd afterwards, shaking their hands and listening to how much they enjoyed what you talked about.

Relax, breathe and open your eyes. Enjoy the feeling of giving a successful speech, or whatever situation it was that you decided to rehearse.

Repeat as often as you can until you feel confident you can do it for real.

The Power Of Two Simple Things

Pen and paper. Writing things down works. The same goes for drawing or creating collages of things you want to achieve or attract into your life. It is as if the act of getting an idea out of your head and into black and white (or glorious color) gives it energy and shows your subconscious that you are taking things seriously. It makes it real.

We have already looked at how powerful your brain is. It should come as little surprise that the act of writing or drawing your dreams and goals triggers a part of your brain called the reticular activating system (RAS). Apart from governing wakefulness and sleep, the RAS acts like a kind of filter for all the information that you are exposed to every day, from the neighbor's overloud music to the taste of your lunchtime sandwich. We are constantly bombarded with this data, in fact some have said we are exposed to more information per day than a 15th century person was exposed to in their whole life.

"The brain processes 400 billion bits of information a second but we are only aware of 2000 of those," says chiropractor, researcher and author Dr. Joseph Dispenza. In order to stop our brains being overwhelmed with information the RAS filters the data, only allowing in what it considers important. And how does the brain decide what is important? It uses as a guideline the stuff that you focus on most. So, if you decide that you want to buy a red Ferrari, suddenly you start seeing them everywhere. It's not that they have magically started to appear (although that could be true!), it's that you have told your brain: *"red Ferraris are important to me,"* and so where it once ignored them, it now notices them. This also works in reverse. If you are constantly focusing on things that are negative, such as *"I'm not a confident person,"* then the brain will try and find ways to show you this is correct. There's a lot of truth in the old saying *"Be careful what you wish for."*

If you focus on what you want by writing, coloring, collaging or drawing, the RAS will show you examples of your goal all around you, alert you to opportunities, make you aware of the tiniest events that could lead to bigger things. In short, putting pen to paper is powerful stuff.

By the way, handwriting is best rather than on a keyboard

for this. When you handwrite something, it activates the brain's reading circuit, a different and more creative part of your gray matter.

Some writing ideas to try

- Write a "shopping list" of things you would like to have in your life
- Write a letter from your future self to yourself now, describing what life is now like and how you have everything in life you imagined
- Carry around a memo pad at all times and write down any thoughts or ideas
- Write a diary or journal every morning and record any insights that are important
- Write down your dreams every morning and see what you make of the symbols
- Write down every good and positive thing that happens to you.
- Write out inspirational quotations
- Write out affirmations, making sure you use the present tense so your brain thinks it is real now. (Not *"I will be self-confident soon,"* but *"I am a self-confident person."*)

Some collage/drawing ideas to try

Make a treasure map. Get some card or colored paper and starting in the center write **MY GOALS** and then draw lines outwards like the spokes of a wheel. At the end of each of these spokes write a category of your life, for example: Health, Work, Free Time, Love and Romance, Family, Spiritual, Creativity … whatever categories you like really. Get a pile of old magazines and cut out pictures that represent your goals and aspirations in each category and stick them on the paper in the appropriate place. Take this treasure map out every day and imagine you have all the things pictured there. Feel what it is like with all your senses. Make it real.

Draw a sketch of you now in a situation you are having issues with, make it as funny as you want. Really pile on the agony! For example, when worried about confidence, draw a "scaredy cat you" hiding in the corner at a party or a "terrified you" concealing yourself under the table in a restaurant when meeting a new date. Now draw the future confident you, who has no problems at all in these kind of situations. For more about this check out a great Ted Talk "Draw your Future" by comedian and motivational speaker Patty Dobrowolski.

Jim Carrey and the Magic Check

Multi-millionaire actor, writer and comedian Jim Carrey believes in visualization. He is living proof it works. He used the power of imagery many years ago as a motivational tool. Back in the mid-1980s, when he was a poor and penniless unknown actor, he would go up on Mulholland Drive in Hollywood, California every night and park. Then, as he told Oprah Winfrey in an interview: *"I would visualize directors interested in me and people I respected saying 'I like your work' and I would visualize things coming to me that I wanted or whatever."* He explained that it made him feel better. *"I would drive home and think well, I do have these things and they're out there, I just don't have a hold of them yet, but they're out there."*

Carrey didn't stop there. At the beginning of the 1990s, he wrote himself a check for $10 million for "Acting Services Rendered" dated Thanksgiving 1995 and gave himself five years to make it happen. He carried it around in his wallet and the more he pulled it out and looked at it, the more dilapidated it got. But he found out, just before Thanksgiving 1995, that *"I was going to make $10 million on Dumb and Dumber."* Powerful proof that when you can imagine something strongly and persistently enough it **can** happen.

Carrey is also quick to point out that you do need to do the work as well. *"You can't just visualize and go eat a sandwich!"*

The Future You Want & How To Get It

A very interesting technique using the power of the imagination and imagery is Imagework, which was pioneered by writer, coach and psychotherapist Dr. Dina Glouberman. On her website, she writes about it like this: *"Everything that you create in your life, from an omelette to a multi-national company to a love affair, begins as an image in your mind. These images are often unconscious and may even originate in very early childhood."*

Imagework teaches you how to access these images and understand them better. All you need do is relax, think of a question or issue and then simply allow an image to enter your mind. Then you work with it to see what it is telling you. You can guide the imagework by having two chairs facing each other. First sit in one as you see the image and then literally move to the other one to ask yourself questions. Why not try it? Let's start with a situation where you need confidence, but don't usually have it. Think of a situation like this now. Maybe it's asking for a raise, or going to a party, or telling your partner you don't like their behavior.

Invite an image to come into your mind which symbolizes

this situation. You might see a small child fighting a lion, or a scared gladiator in the middle of an area surrounded by baying crowds. Don't force it, just see what image arises. You can step inside the image and see how it feels. Imagine it as fully as you can. If you want you can speak out loud and record your comments on your phone. Switch chairs and ask yourself to give you an image for how to improve the situation.

Return to your original chair and let an image enter your mind which improves the situation, describe what you see, get inside the image or look at it from a distance.

What insights have you got from doing this? Write them in your notebook. Continue for as long as is useful.

One very interesting way to work with images is to imagine that a situation is in the future and already as you want it to be, a dream scenario if you like, and then ask yourself how you achieved it. Let's do this now, with the same situation as above, but now you feel super confident and happy with the way you are dealing with things.

Form an image in your mind which shows a "future you" dealing successfully with a situation that would normally make you feel overwhelmed and afraid.

Really feel what this positive situation at some point in the future is like. Get as much into the image as you can. What is your future self doing and saying? How do you look and feel?

Imagine your future self could give your present self some advice about how he or she got to this happy and successful place. What does your future self say?

Meeting Your Heroes

Using your imagination and visualizing positive things gets even more interesting if you invite a celebrity from the past, present or future to join you! What's even more fun is that they can be a real person, or a fictitious character from a film or book.

We can all think of people who, for us, symbolize and epitomize a particular quality or skill. For example, if you had to choose someone who summed up all the qualities of a successful entrepreneur, you might choose Bill Gates or Steve Jobs or someone completely different, like your father's friend John. Who would you think of first if you had to express the quality of compassion? Maybe Mother Teresa or Princess Diana or Florence Nightingale? You get the idea.

Think of a situation you need to deal with which requires a particular character trait or personal quality or skill. Who would be the ideal person to advise you? Don't hold back, you can choose anyone in the world. I like calling on Albert Einstein when I need to apply a bit of intelligence to a situation, Sherlock Holmes if something needs investigating and William Shakespeare for help with writing.

In your mind's eye, go to a calm and tranquil place and wait for the person to appear. If you can't see them clearly then get a sense that they are there. Believe they are with you. Ask your question or explain your problem and wait for an answer. Maybe they will use words or actions or point you towards an object or image. Thank them and say goodbye. Don't worry, you can meet them again any time you want. Open your eyes and write down any insights in your notebook.

Three Doors

This is one of my favorite visualization exercises and I use it a lot to get insight into situations or to choose between different solutions to a problem. It can be applied to confidence by asking the right questions before you open the doors. Let me explain how it works.

- Think of the situation, problem or decision you need insight about.

- Come up with three different scenarios. For example, if you are not sure if you are confident enough to ask for a raise then the three options could be: a) ask for a raise, b) don't ask for a raise c) do something else other than ask

- Close your eyes and relax. Imagine you are standing in front of three closed doors. Each door represents one of the options you thought of. Look how different they are.

- In your mind's eye stand in front of the first door. Remember what it represents. Describe it from the outside. How big is it? What color is it? Is it well cared for or dilapidated? Is it old or new? What is it made of?

- When you are ready, open the door and describe the first thing you see. Continue to move inside the door and describe everything, what you see, how you feel, whether you want to stay or go. Come back out when you are ready and close the door behind you.

- Repeat the same thing for doors 2 and 3.

- Either write about this in your notebook or just think about what you saw behind each door.

- What can you take away from this? Do any of the options seem clearer?

Chapter 5 Key Take-Aways

In this chapter, we have looked at:

- How athletes and musicians use visualization, employing as many of the sense as possible to recover from injury and improve performance.

- How it doesn't matter if you are not good at "visualizing".

- The power of visualizing a positive experience bringing it to life by really imagining with all your senses.

- The importance of writing, drawing and collage and how the Reticular Activating System works.

- A list of different techniques which involve applying pen to paper or glue to pictures.

- How Jim Carrey visualized his way to a successful multi-million-dollar career.

- How to use images to get insight into a current situation.

- How to create a successful "future you" who can tell you how they did it.

- Asking famous people, dead or alive, real or fictitious, for advice using the power of our imagination.

- The three doors technique and how it can give you insight into a situation or decision.

The power of imagery and visualization is incredible. Your mind can do amazing things if you harness its abilities. But it needs to happen in more than just your head. That's what the next chapter is about. Taking action and faking it 'til you make it. So, get ready, it's going to be fun!

Chapter 6 – How To Easily…Just Do It, Even If It Scares You

"You are what you believe yourself to be."
Paulo Coelho

It is time for some tough love. You are going to have to go out and do the things that scare you, otherwise reading this book is simply just a waste of time.

Your brain is your powerhouse. We have already seen how it doesn't distinguish between real and imagined events. We have also learned that it can develop new neural pathways when things are repeated often enough. The trouble is, this can work both ways, good and bad. Negative self-talk is like a self-fulfilling prophecy.

If you tell yourself: *"I'm just no good at meeting new people, I always make a fool of myself,"* then your brain will accept that as true and look for evidence to show that is the case. You will drop something, you will forget what you're saying and then reinforce the negativity by saying out loud or to yourself: *"Well, how typical of me! I knew I was a clumsy idiot. This just proves it!"*

It turns into a vicious circle of negativity. You will feel under constant stress as you encounter more and more situations where you may make a fool of yourself. Your sympathetic nervous system is triggered as your body puts you in fight-or-flight mode. Toxic stress chemicals wash through you, increasing your heart rate and breathing, making your mouth dry and your knees turn to jelly. All because of what you believe is true.

Fortunately, this can work to your benefit as well. You can

convince your brain that good things are true, even if they are not real, and then experience positive effects. Let's take a familiar example.

The placebo effect is a well-known phenomenon in medicine. Someone is told they are getting a drug that will cure their illness. Then they are given something harmless which has no medical properties at all. (The doctor might inject them with distilled water or give them a sugar pill, for example.) The curious thing is that their symptoms will usually improve. Sometimes, this effect has been powerful enough to cause cancerous tumors to disappear. And more curiously, this works even when the person knows they are taking a placebo! What is going on? No actual medicine has been administered, so how can the person be improving or even cured?

Researchers believe a combination of nurturing (by the healthcare professional or person administering the placebo) and relaxation (from feeling something is being done and may work), switches off the "stress chemicals", including cortisol, norepinephrine and epinephrine (adrenaline), which have been activated because of the illness. Instead, the body's natural healing hormones: oxytocin, dopamine, nitrous oxide and endorphins swoosh through, calming you down, slowing your racing heart, lowering your blood pressure and restoring your breathing. This in turn allows the immune system to fight the illness. No wonder placebos make people feel better.

What has this to do with faking it 'til you make it? Because in a sense you are creating your own placebo effect. By acting in a confident way, you are showing your mind that it doesn't have to be in a state of stress. There's nothing to worry about! You have it all handled.
In order to fake it, you have got to have a model to imitate.

Let's study the body language, breathing and attitude of a self-confident person and then copy them. Looking the part is half the battle. But there is more to it than that, you'll discover something rather clever will be going on in your body as you do this, meaning things may not be quite as fake as you think.

The Body Language of Confidence & Assertiveness

Being self-confident is partly to do with what goes on inside your head, we know that. But a large part of it goes on outside your head. It includes how you appear to other people. This means:

- body language including facial expression and eye contact
- breathing
- voice
- dress

Let's examine the body language of a confident person. Think of someone you know. Someone you consider self-confident. How do they appear to you? See them in your mind's eye and study how they stand and walk, their facial expression, and how they use their eyes and hands.

It may seem like an obvious cause and effect. A confident person will automatically have confident body language. But did you know that positioning your body in a particular way, even if you feel shy inside, can actually make you feel more confident. That's interesting, isn't it? Studies show that if you stand or move in a certain way, it will make you feel that way! Back in the 19th century Charles Darwin was definitely onto something when he said: *"Even the simulation of an emotion tends to arouse it in our minds."*

Take something as simple as smiling. Children smile up to 400 times a day, whereas 14 percent of adults don't even manage five smiles a day. Smiling makes you feel better. Among other things, it affects brain chemistry, releasing our favorite relaxing hormones: dopamine, endorphins and so on. Smilers have been shown to live longer and have happier lives. Smiling has a good effect on others too, as research has shown people who smile are seen as friendly, approachable and competent. (Competent! That's an unexpected one, isn't it?) There's a great Ted Talk on this by entrepreneur Ron Gutman, definitely worth a look. If you are trying to build confidence then the message is obvious. Smile!

Mom Was Right!

If you were told to sit up straight when you were a kid, then your Mom or teacher was giving you very good advice. Confident people don't slouch or hold their heads down. They don't fold their arms across their bodies or stand with their weight on one leg. These are all classic body language messages conveying weakness.

What do confident people look like?

- Their weight is evenly distributed on both legs
- Their back is straight
- Their chin is level
- Their shoulders are back
- Their arms are by their sides
- They make eye contact

This is confident body language. It sends a message that you have a stable foundation *(weight on both legs),* and can't be pushed around *(how easy is it to push over someone with their weight on one leg?)* It shows you are open to being approached *(arms by sides, eye contact)* and that you consider yourself on an equal footing with everyone in the room *(you are not trying to make yourself look smaller by stooping or looking down.)*

The great thing about imitating one or more of these body positions is that it alters your subconscious. You will literally feel stronger and more confident. It creates new neural pathways, which will feel strange and awkward at first, but will also empower you. The more you focus your attention on deliberately using one or more of those "confident" gestures, the more comfortable you will feel, so don't give up.

Every Breath You Take

Confident people breathe evenly at regular to slow speed with little upper chest movement. That's what you want to achieve and copy.

When someone is nervous, anxious or stressed, lots of things are happening in the body. We've already discussed the fight-or-flight response and the toxic cocktail of chemicals that are sloshing around your body if this "threat" is not dealt with quickly. The stress response also affects heart rate, blood pressure and breathing. Stressed people breathe much more quickly from the upper chest and take more breaths. The greater the feeling of stress, the faster you breathe and the more you try and get gulps of air. This over-breathing can cause you to feel dizzy, light-headed and faint.

There are several different breathing techniques you can use to help you feel less stressed and more in control. In other words, to breathe more like a confident person. I'm going to introduce you to one approach to breathing called the **Buteyko Method**. The objective of this method is to *"maintain the correct ratio of oxygen and carbon dioxide within the bloodstream."*

Professor Konstantin Buteyko, a Russian medical scientist, developed a technique of breathing which resulted in the perfect way for a healthy adult to breathe: *"lightly, superficially and only through the nose."* This may be a surprise to you as often to help with stress we are encouraged to take deep breaths. Buteyko's method is based on the principal that most people, including those with asthma, breathe too deeply. This causes an imbalance in the ratio of carbon dioxide to oxygen in the blood, because when we over-breathe, we take in too much oxygen and lose valuable carbon dioxide.

Rhythm is crucial to optimal breathing, you can change your physiology if you breathe in a fixed rhythm and in a smooth, soft way. It will activate your parasympathetic nervous system and relax you. If you are relaxed then you will feel more self-confident.

Easily Finding Your Confident Voice

If you are nervous, strange things happen to your voice. It may be faint, or squeaky or faltering. You may not even be able to get your words out at all or they come out too fast. That is because in a stressed state, the frontal lobes of the brain shut down in order to conserve energy! You don't need a huge amount of brainpower when you are running from a hungry tiger, your energy is best spent helping you run faster or fight harder!

Because your brain isn't really working properly if you are

stressed, your voice goes peculiar. Confident people don't seem to have this problem, do they? A confident person's voice is well-modulated, they speak slowly and clearly. How can you do that too?

Basically you want to make sure your voice comes from your chest and not your throat. Singers learn how to do this. You need to breathe from your diaphragm. There are exercises you can do to help you develop a stronger voice, from humming to laughing, so take a look at YouTube or Google "voice exercises".

Speak louder than you think you need to. This is particularly true for giving speeches and talks. Practice with a friend who will tell you if you are talking loudly enough.

Don't let your voice rise at the end of sentences or phrases, except if asking a question. There is a common trend to add rising intonation to everything that you say, so that even a statement sounds like a question. Great speakers don't do this. Confident people don't do this. Their voices stay level or go down at the end of statements.

Speak more slowly than you think you need to. When we're nervous we tend to gabble, slow it down and give yourself time to think.

Dress

You know the saying *"you don't judge a book by its cover"*? Believe me, it's **not** true. When people meet you for the first time, they are definitely judging how you look.

If you dress the part, you will automatically feel more confident. Making sure that what you wear fits well, is clean and immaculate is a given, but there's more to it than looking neat and tidy. Choose an outfit that makes you feel your best, that is "you", but that is also suitable for the occasion and the audience you will be facing.

Now, don't get me wrong. I'm not saying that you should lose your sense of personal style and just wear conservative and boring clothes. But wearing something that is deliberately different and unusual in a particular context, like a red leather rock chick outfit to a new client meeting with your law firm, takes a certain degree of confidence and attitude. It's great if you can carry it off, but if you have that amount of confidence already, you probably don't need to be reading this book! You want to feel relaxed and happy with the image you are presenting to the world. If you are stylish, smart and are decked out in something that flatters you and that you enjoy wearing, your confidence will soar!

Different colors suit different people, so a very good investment of your time is to discover "your" colors. Although wearing the shades that make you look great is a huge bonus, this is not just a confidence thing. It saves money as you only buy clothes that are in your range of colors, and all your outfits will go together easily if they are in the same color palette.
There are various ways you can find out the colors that suit you. Try Googling *"How to find colors that suit me"* or a similar phrase. There's a ton of stuff out there. One simple basic step is to determine what your skin undertone is. Look at the veins on the inside of your wrist. If they appear blue or purple, you have cool undertones, if they appear green then you have warm undertones.

As a very rough guide, cool undertoned people tend to look best in:

- black
- white
- blue
- gray
- navy
- silvery metallics.

Warm undertoned people look best in:
- coral
- burnt orange
- cream
- brown
- yellow
- warm red
- gold, copper or bronze metallics.

There is a bit more to it than just skin undertone of course, there's eye and hair color to consider as well, but it's a good first step.

Another very simple and fun way to decide what colors look best on you is to invite a friend over, (or do this on your own), and try on lots of different colored tops or scarves. These should be next to your face and a single solid color. Then just see what makes your hair, skin and eyes glow. The difference between a "good" and a "bad" color for you can be quite astonishing.

Role Models

Motivational speaker Jim Rohn once famously said that the five people you spend most time with has a profound influence on who you are. Successful self-help author and businessman Tim Ferriss is a great believer in this rule. When asked what he would print on a billboard, that was what he chose. Some people are fortunate enough to have great role models in their life, but many of us don't. The five people we most associate with may not necessarily be the best ones for our self-esteem and self-confidence. But you may not be able to do much about that, if they are family members or work colleagues.

What you can do is to choose a well-known mentor and then immerse yourself in their books, talks and YouTube videos. A lot of people already do this with pop celebrities, but that is probably not the best choice. Liking someone's music or fashion style is one thing, using them as a motivational example of how to live your life and be your best self is quite another.

Spend some time thinking of the kind of qualities you want to develop and improve. Self-confidence is probably going to be one of those. Do a bit of internet research and see if you can find an author or teacher or business executive who demonstrates those qualities and has lots online. Just as an aside, I am not talking about spending money enrolling on an online course run by a so-called guru. I am talking about a person who has overcome shyness or some other disadvantage and lived a successful life. If you would like the name of one of my personal favorites, try researching Helen Keller and prepare to be amazed. Read, watch, or listen to a little bit of wisdom from this person every day, even for just a few minutes and you will start to absorb some of their attitudes and their mindset. They can be one of your five people you spend most time with. Add more people if you need to.

How Would the Most Confident Person in the World Behave?

Teacher trainer Fionnula Wilson had to give a lecture to a small group of teachers in Italy a few years ago. This is what happened and how she handled it:

"They had moved me to the stage because of the number of people who had turned up. There were at least 80 teachers sitting in front of me and I had material for 20. Everything I had planned so carefully would have to be abandoned. I smiled at the audience while my brain flew into overdrive. How could I manage this situation without looking a complete idiot?

At this point I decided to use a strategy that has always helped me when I am scared. I said to myself: How would the most confident person in the world handle this situation?

In my mind's eye, Superteacher appeared. She was wearing a black sequined academic gown, sparkly mortar board and a red and blue leotard. Superteacher was beautiful with the IQ of a genius and a razor-sharp wit. To mirror her confidence, all I had to do was step into her high silver boots. I imagined how Superteacher stood, and copied it, pulled my shoulders back, lifted my head up. She's great at eye contact, so I took my time and looked round the audience with a calm smile.

Superteacher has an amazing voice, so I walked forward to the middle of the stage and greeted the audience clearly and confidently. I put my lesson plan on the chair. Suddenly I knew what I was going to do with this group. I told them about the power of the mind and my belief that confidence could be channeled. Then I told them about my experience the previous night. I had just arrived, I didn't know anyone and I was hungry but I didn't want to go into a restaurant and eat on my own. As I talked I mimed how I felt, making my body smaller, turning my shoulders in. I put them in pairs and asked them to act out the scene. One was the waiter or waitress and the other a lonely, hungry, self-conscious customer. We spread out a bit as I wanted people on their feet. I told the waiting staff to be patronizing and arrogant, the customers to be super shy.

I walked round the hall. The "customers" spoke in faint apologetic voices, their body language was inward-focused, they looked at the floor. The waiters and waitresses smirked and looked condescending. They swapped over roles just to make it fair and then I went back onto the stage. We all agreed the self-consciousness and embarrassment of dining alone was horrible.

Then, I asked them to tell me how the most confident person in the world would act in the same situation. As their suggestions came, I did as they told me. I stood up straight, I looked round the room. I was now a Very Confident Customer.

We redid the role-play. But this time, the teachers playing the customer were channeling their confident personas. The volume in the room went up. Their eyes sparkled, they ordered pretend wine and drank it in a relaxed way as they looked around the "restaurant." Some sent their waiters away as they wanted some time to decide what to order. One or two people asked to change tables. It was wonderful. I asked them if they felt different and of course they did. "But you're the same person," I said. "You just decided to act confidently. And then, magically, while you are acting, it becomes real. You can use this for all kinds of things you're scared of."

One asked me if I had really done that last night. I said yes. In my mind, Superteacher smiled and nodded her head. She had doubled as Supercustomer the night before.

"Your mind is tremendously powerful. You always have a choice. You can let fear and stress stop you from doing things, or you can act as if you are confident. And when you're confident – even if you're just pretending – anything can happen!"

When everyone had left, I tidied up my unused handouts and looked round the empty room. 'That went well,' said Superteacher in my head.

"Couldn't have done it without you," I replied.

Chapter 6 Key Take-Aways

In this chapter, we have looked at:

- The power of the placebo effect and how it may impact faking it 'til you make it.

- What confidence looks like in terms of body language, breathing, voice and dress.

- The importance of a good role model.

- Asking yourself how the most confident person in the world would do something and then copying that.

The next chapter takes things to the next level as we look at the incredible power of happiness and gratitude. It's a game changer.

Chapter 7 – Self-Esteem and Happiness

"Gratitude is not only the greatest of virtues, but the parent of all others."
Marcus Tullius Cicero

Happiness and self-esteem are closely linked. Both are experienced in our minds and not necessarily related to external circumstances. You may be wealthy and have status, but be deeply unhappy. On the other hand, as studies of primitive peoples have shown, it is perfectly possible to have a high level of self-esteem and be very happy without the material trappings of an enormous salary, a designer wardrobe and a prestigious job.

Happiness and self-esteem feed off and nurture each other. If you feel good about yourself and are fulfilling your wants and needs, you are more likely to be happy. If you are feeling happy, the chances are your self-confidence and self-esteem will be higher. Of course, this works the other way around. Low self-esteem often leads to unhappiness, while being depressed and feeling down will have a negative impact on how confident you feel. It therefore seems a good idea that if you want to work on achieving a healthy level of self-esteem, you should work on your happiness.

If it sounds bizarre to think you can "work on" your happiness like you can work on your abs, then think again. A whole new area of psychology has emerged recently devoted to studying what makes us happy and how we can get more of it. Called positive psychology, it uses an avalanche of research and peer-reviewed resources to show the positive effects of happiness. It has been shown that happy people perform better, are more intelligent, more creative and more successful than unhappy ones. What's not to love?

The happiness that helps us is not the transitory kind, the kind you get when you dive headfirst into a tub of chocolate cookie ice cream or win $100 in the lottery. It is long term and can survive life's ups and downs. The kind that is defined by the Ancient Greeks, and quoted by positive psychologist Shawn Achor in his book The Happiness Advantage, as "the joy we feel striving after our potential."

It's worth mentioning at this point that there is a difference between having a positive outlook on life, being a "glass half full" type of person, and being recklessly optimistic. Thinking everything is going to have a happy outcome regardless of the circumstances can be as unhealthy as being overly pessimistic. There is even a psychological condition known as the Pollyanna Syndrome, (named after a character in a 1913 novel, who always plays "the glad game"), whose sufferers have unrealistic optimism. This can be dangerous because people may behave recklessly and take unnecessary risks thinking *"it couldn't possibly happen to me"*.

Learning Happiness

With that warning in mind, let's look at how you can learn to be happy. In the UK there are "positive education" methods in schools which teach pupils good practice, such as meditation and gratitude. In the USA (and worldwide online), the University of California has a free eight-week Science of Happiness Course which is the first MOOC (massive open online course) to teach positive psychology.

What steps can you take yourself? Nicky Campbell's radio show on BBC Live 5 talks to Action for Happiness, which states that 40 percent of our happiness results from our "conscious choices."

They list ten ways to become happier:

- Do things for others
- Connect with people
- Take care of your body
- Notice the world around you
- Keep learning new things
- Have goals to look forward to
- Find ways to bounce back from difficulties
- Take a positive approach
- Become comfortable with who you are
- Be part of something bigger which gives you purpose and meaning in life.

Have Some Fun!

If you want to learn happiness, then consider obvious yet overlooked things like play and fun. And if you think you haven't got time or that fun is for children, think again. Having fun is very good for you in more ways than you might imagine.

In his best-selling book Play, medical doctor, psychiatrist and founder of the National Institute for Play, Stuart Brown cites countless examples of people who have benefited from taking a more light-hearted approach to life. As he says: *"there is a kind of magic in play. What might seem like a frivolous or even childish pursuit is ultimately beneficial. It's paradoxical that a little bit of 'non-productive' activity can make one enormously more productive and invigorated in other aspects of life."*

By definition, play is something that gives us great pleasure and time seems to stand still while we are absorbed in it. No-one forces us to do it and there's no pay check. It seems to have no motive or purpose. It also means different things to different people, so making a quilt may be a joyous experience for you but a nightmare activity for someone who needs to be outdoors and playing tennis to have fun. It's highly individual and there's no right or wrong, (although I would dispute that mindlessly surfing the web or going on Facebook is proper "play".)

To put some play back into your life, you can start with something simple and immediately rewarding, like going for a walk or playing with your child or pet. It's hard to be depressed when you are moving and laughing at the antics of a funny child or animal (why do you think all those cute cat clips are so popular on YouTube?)

To take play seriously, you need to transport yourself back to the times in childhood when you were so caught up in what you were doing that you forgot the time, the day and where you were. What activities made you feel like that? If, like me, you spent a lot of your childhood pretending to look after a horse made from an old dustbin with a piece of wood for its head, then maybe you could consider doing some horseback riding now?

The Man Who Laughed Himself Well

In 1964, Norman Cousins was the editor-in-chief of the Saturday Review in New York city when he was diagnosed with an incurable and fatal condition called Ankylosing Spondylitis and given a few months to live.

As a journalist, Cousins was used to research and so set about finding out as much as he could about his condition. He knew it had happened just after a very stressful trip to

Russia and so he concluded that his emotions had a lot to do with his illness. As a result, he rejected the colossal negativity of the doctors and being told what to do by the medical profession and so checked himself out of hospital and into a hotel. He believed vitamin C was key and so had massive doses of it injected daily. But the most interesting thing was that to lift his mood, he watched funny movies every day, laughing until he hurt, for a month. He later said that ten minutes of belly-aching laughter would allow him two hours of pain free sleep, something morphine couldn't achieve.

Norman Cousins died in 1990, 26 years after his fatal diagnosis. He wrote a number of non-fiction books about health, including the best-selling 1979 book Anatomy of an Illness. This was a groundbreaking work because it looked at illness from a layman's point of view and discussed, for almost the first time, the concept of patients taking control of their own health.

It can't be proved conclusively that laughter made the difference to Norman Cousins, but it certainly didn't do any harm!

The Power of Gratitude

One amazing and very simple thing you can do to increase your level of happiness and experience all kinds of other positive benefits relatively quickly is to start practicing gratitude. What does practicing gratitude actually involve? We discussed it a little bit earlier in the book. It means being thankful on a regular basis and expressing that thanks in words or writing in an aware and thoughtful manner.

You are probably used to showing gratitude when you get a

gift or someone does something nice for you. You may even have written a thank you note or sent a card to show your appreciation. However, practicing gratitude in the way that builds happiness and confidence means being thankful every day, or several times a day, without having a reason. It makes you actively look around you and value all the things in your life that are normally taken for granted, like sunshine and rain, having a roof over your head, not living in a war zone, having clean water to drink and being able to read and write.

These may seem very simple, even banal, things to focus on, but positive psychology research has shown that grateful people sleep better and are healthier both physically and psychologically. Gratitude is a great stress buster too. In fact, a 2006 study in Behavior Research and Therapy conducted with Vietnam War veterans showed a lower rate of PTSD (post-traumatic stress disorder) amongst those with higher levels of gratitude. Grateful people are less aggressive and have increased feelings of well-being, peace and self-esteem. In other words, they feel happier! They are also less likely to be materialistic and more likely to be social too. Oh, and in case you need more evidence, grateful people live longer!

Gratitude Lists and Journals

It's good to write down things you are thankful for. A list, a journal, a letter to yourself. And here's the proof!

The Emmons Lab, under the direction of Dr. Robert Emmons, Professor of Psychology at the UC Davis, California is engaged in *"a long-term research project designed to research and disseminate a large body of scientific data on the nature of gratitude, its causes, and its potential consequences for human health and well-being."*

They have published a large amount of research material to back up the positive effects of gratitude and are currently focusing on the development of gratitude in children.

They have discovered that people keeping weekly *"gratitude journals"* took more regular exercise and generally felt more optimistic about what might be coming up in the next week than those who didn't. They were also more likely to have moved forward on the achievement of personal goals.

Keeping a gratitude journal or simply listing the things you are grateful for on a regular basis is simple, free and has proven scientific effects. It's kind of a no-brainer really. Why not give it a try now? Write down ten things that you are grateful for in your life.

Paying it Forward

Closely linked to gratitude is kindness, but while you can practice gratitude in private on your own, kindness tends to be a more public affair, or at least involve some social interaction. I love the concept of random acts of kindness. You know – a small and anonymous gesture, like paying the toll for the person behind you on the turnpike or for a stranger's coffee in the coffee shop. It needn't involve money, you can help someone to cross the street or help them lift their shopping onto the bus.

Trying to do one random act of kindness every day has lots of benefits and not just for the recipient. It takes your attention off yourself, something self-conscious people find hard to do. Research has also shown it has a positive effect on your health, particularly for very socially anxious people. It seems that doing something nice for someone releases our old friend oxytocin, one of the hormones that helps you feel calm and happy.

If you need any inspiration for how to be randomly kind, then just type "random acts of kindness" or "pay it forward" into Google. Even if you don't end up doing anything (and I hope you do!) you are bound to be inspired by just how many great and thoughtful people there are out there. Here is just one small example to keep you going:

On October 29, 2012, the storm surge from Hurricane Sandy hit New York City. Numerous people were left without power and because contacting family and friends via cell phone was so important, this meant thousands couldn't charge their phones and tell loved ones they were safe. Several families who still had power ran extension cords out to the street and invited people to use the power for free to charge their phones. It was just one of many acts of kindness during this devastating event.

Enjoying Confidence

It's been proven many times that actively training yourself to have a positive outlook can affect all aspects of your life, including your confidence. Regardless of what situation you find yourself in, if you can be calm and see the humor, if you can focus on other people more than yourself, if you can show gratitude instead of looking for something to complain about then you will have created a sound foundation. You will be working from a position of strength and not be tossed about by your emotions.

When you're in a state of flow, completely involved in an activity for its own sake, you are being truly authentic, living in the moment and not worrying about what people think of you, how you look or how confident you seem. It's a great feeling and one that it's worth aspiring too.

Make no mistake, deciding to be happy, grateful and kind does take work. It's all too easy to fall back into bad habits. You need to train yourself to do it and you need to check in several times a day to make sure you are always doing your best. This may sound calculating and artificial, after all, if you feel pissed off you feel pissed off, right? Why pretend to look on the bright side if you really want to stay in bed all day under the covers and hide?

Remember we talked in the last chapter about acting "as if" about "faking it 'til you make it"? It doesn't just apply to modeling yourself on a successful person or imagining what the most confident person in the world would do. It also means acting in as positive a way as you can, smiling and choosing to be optimistic even if you feel like doing the complete opposite.

If you have a problem with confidence and self-esteem, then you have already spent a long time learning to be anxious and looking on the black side. It may not seem like that, but it's true. You have spent so long acting that way that it has become second nature. You have learned to do it well. People feel uncomfortable with change and so being positive and working on your happiness will feel odd at first. But as you persevere it will become easier. They say it takes 30 days for something to become a habit, so why not challenge yourself to a month of positive activities and see how you feel by the end?

One of the most important things you can do is learn to laugh at yourself. Many of the world's most successful comedians were, and are, very shy people who realized they could make people laugh. No-one really enjoys spending time with people who take themselves too seriously.

This doesn't mean you need to walk around cracking jokes or entertaining your workmates to half an hour of stand-up every day. Not everyone is that gifted, I'm certainly not! But if you are talking to someone and they ask you how you are, think before you speak. Don't launch into a monologue about the awful day you have had, how terrible your boss is, how the phone bill was twice what it should be, your dog looks sick and you are worried that you might get mugged on the way home. That sounds like an exaggeration, but I know a few people just like that! As my dear mother used to say: *"You ask them how they are and they tell you!"*

Why not focus on the good or amusing things that have happened to you instead? Laugh about how you got caught in the rain and your new hairstyle made you look like a drowned rat! Life's too short not to see the funny side.

If you really are struggling with this then do what Norman Cousins did. Watch some funny films on YouTube and laugh 'til your tummy hurts!

Chapter 7 Key Take-Aways
In this chapter, we have looked at:

- The link between happiness and self-esteem.

- How you can work on your happiness.

- Positive psychology and what it can teach us.

- The power of fun and play.

- The man who laughed himself well.

- How to practice gratitude.

- Kindness and paying it forward.

- How to enjoy confidence.

So far, we have studied the effects the mind can have on confidence, but did you know there are some physical ways to affect how you feel. That maybe by tapping points on your face or touching an anchor on your arm you can instantly feel confident? Intrigued? I bet you are, so let's take a look!

Chapter 8 - Body Language, EFT and NLP

"There is more wisdom in your body than in your deepest philosophy."
Friedrich Nietzsche

How well do you know your own body? I don't mean the outside, we all know our own lumps and bumps intimately. I mean the *inside*. Because your body is speaking to you all the time, you just need to learn how to listen.

In Chapter 6 we looked at the importance of body language. To recap briefly, gestures, the way you stand and the way you move all speak volumes. It's easy to spot a confident person or a shy person in a group without listening to a word they say, simply by observing how they are occupying the space they are in.

Confident people have their weight on both feet, shoulders back and head up. They hold their hands by their sides or use gestures freely and they move around a space easily, maintaining good eye contact with whoever they are talking to. On the other hand, a person low in self-esteem or lacking confidence will try to make themselves as inconspicuous as possible within their space. They may stay in the corner or the shadows. They will turn in on themselves, look down, touch themselves on the arm or chest as if to give themselves a hug, have their weight unevenly distributed and avoid catching anyone's eye.

It's such a fascinating subject and if you're interested in learning more, then why not type something like "body language" or "confident body language" into the search box in YouTube and see what kind of stuff comes up. If you try out just one or two ideas it can make a difference, so why not give it a go?

In this chapter, we're going to look at a different kind of body language. You'll learn how your body speaks to you and how to use various techniques and bodywork to build confidence.

Tuning In To Your Body

If you take the time to tune in, you'll find that your body is constantly providing you with information about your feelings, emotions and health. Many people tune these messages out and distract themselves with food, alcohol, work, surfing the internet… any manner of things that will divert attention from what your body is trying to tell you.

Lots of people blot out feelings of thirst, tiredness, stress or chronic pain. You get so used to feeling constantly exhausted, for example, that it becomes your default position. Or you find that you've gone an entire day without drinking any plain water at all, just tea, coffee, soda or alcohol. It's not that you weren't thirsty, you just don't recognize the feeling anymore because you've ignored it so often. Or maybe you spend most days sitting in a room in front of a computer, not realizing that your body is crying out for movement, fresh air and nature. Getting back in touch with your body helps establish a feeling of calm confidence which is obvious to others. There are several ways to tune back in:

Get into the habit of scanning your body, that is, take a few moments several times a day to mentally check yourself over from top to bottom and see how you are feeling.

Are you cold? Hungry? Do you have a dry mouth? You will be amazed at how much information your body is giving you.

Get out in nature. When was the last time you went for a walk in the countryside? Spending time outside helps you in all kinds of ways, from getting more oxygen into your system to releasing those feel-good neurotransmitters like serotonin. It's been proved to increase feelings of well-being and improve concentration too. You might like to read up on a theory called grounding, which encourages you to go barefoot on the earth. It's based on the premise that the earth is more negatively charged than your body and so you absorb earth's electrons which have an anti-inflammatory effect, grounding has been nick-named "earth's antioxidant."

Have a massage. What better way to put you back in touch with your body than having a massage? Apart from the obvious fact that it is relaxing and can ease muscle tension, massage also helps you sleep better, boosts your immune system and helps with anxiety and depression.

Move! Research has shown that movement aids depression and increases energy levels. Scientists have already found that people with mild to medium depressive disorders very often have sedentary lifestyles. There is even a way they describe the position very many of us work in. I am sure you know that slumped position in front of the screen? It's called the *"collapsed sit"* and is actually linked to depression. The way to counteract that, and give yourself a serotonin boost is to **move**. Walk, dance, run, do some yoga or Qigong, go ride a horse...it doesn't really matter too much, the important thing is to just get out of that chair!

Write a little bit. It can be really effective to spend a few minutes every day simply writing down exactly how your body feels, bit by bit. Is your mouth dry? What can you smell, or is your nose blocked? Do your eyes feel clear and relaxed … and so on.

Decide if you need to rest. While scanning your body, check how tired you are. Do you need to take a nap or lie down for a few minutes? This is particularly important if you are not getting enough sleep at night. Your body needs some time to recharge and will send you signals – some subtle, some not so subtle – that it needs to relax.

Pay attention to your appetite. Many of us eat out of habit when we aren't really hungry, so check if that applies to you. This works in reverse too, you may have got used to skipping meals and are suppressing any food cravings by having a cigarette or a drink or doing extra work? Try to pay attention to what happens to your body after you eat something. There may be some foods that have a negative effect on you, but you haven't yet noticed. There is a well-known link between sugar intake and depression. Psychology Today cites research which shows *"heavy sugar consumption to an increased risk of depression."* They go on to say: *"countries with a high sugar intake also have a high rate of depression."* Food for thought!

Regulate what you drink. During the few moments when you are scanning your body, tune in to whether or not you are thirsty. This is something a lot of people just ignore until they get a dry mouth and feel dehydrated. Drinking water regularly during the day is good for you, not gulping it down like someone who has just come across an oasis in the Sahara, but sipping slowly. Beware of fruit juices and colas which can flood your body with sugar and give you a quick high then a crashing low. The same goes for alcohol.

A small glass of wine or beer with a meal is fine and the occasional celebration won't do you any harm. But regular drinking is bad for your body and will make you more depressed and tired. Alcohol initially helps you crash out, but then makes you snap awake after a few hours. This is because of the "rebound effect" - the body tries to restore a normal sleep pattern as it clears alcohol from your system but tends to go too much the other way and wakes you up instead. They say one drink may help you sleep (until you get used to it) but more than one isn't such a good idea if you want a good night's shut eye.

Body Talk

Once you have started listening to your body more closely, you can try this exercise. Get comfortable then relax deeply, using whatever method usually works for you. Now, think of something that you feel very confident doing. This does not have to be a big deal, it could be training the dog, playing tennis, writing a letter – it's just got to be something you feel you do easily and well.

In your mind's eye, immerse yourself in the experience. You should be quite good at this by now! Really feel as if you are doing it and then study how your body feels, check out your breathing, heart rate, how dry your mouth is, if there is any tension in your muscles and how you feel in the pit of your stomach. This is what confidence feels like.

Now you're going to do something I wouldn't normally advise, which is to picture a situation which scares you or makes you anxious. Again, don't get too extreme, we don't want full-blown terror! Immerse yourself in the situation as much as you can and notice how you are feeling, just as you did before. Make a note that this is what anxiety and

99

discomfort feels like.

Revisit a positive and confidence-building scene to finish the exercise, as you don't want to leave on a negative note.

Do this exercise several times over a few days, until you are totally sure that you can recognize each state easily. Why is this important? Because you can use them as a measure to help you evaluate decisions and situations, to get your "gut feeling" on something.

As an example, let's say you have been offered two jobs which both seem equally good and you are not sure which one to accept. Let your body decide for you. Relax, thinking of each job in turn and "read" your body's reaction. Maybe one of the jobs makes you feel relaxed, happy and strong like you usually do when you're confident while the other creates a tight feeling in your chest and makes your heart hammer like you do when you are anxious. It looks like your body already knows which job is best for you, even if you don't!

Tapping into Success

One method which involves using your body to help with all kinds of issues, including confidence and self-esteem, is the Emotional Freedom Technique or EFT for short.

On the surface, this seems a very curious system. It involves tapping key points on your face and body while focusing on a specific issue. The theory is that tapping on these energy meridian points, (which correspond to some of those used in acupuncture) will release blockages. Although you can use it for health problems, EFT is primarily used for psychological or emotional issues.

The EFT process begins by the person focusing on the issue they want to resolve. They give it a number from zero (no response) to ten (extreme response), depending on how intense the emotional reaction is. Then they repeat an affirmation or series of affirmations while tapping on nine specific points:

- The "karate point", which is the side of the hand under the little finger
- On the eyebrow, directly above the middle of one eye
- The side of the eye
- Under the eye in the middle
- Under the nose
- The middle of the chin
- The clavicle
- Under the armpit
- The crown of the head.

After this the emotional intensity is checked again, using the number scale as before. These rounds of tapping and affirming are repeated until the intensity is at zero.

Some people are quite skeptical of EFT and say there is no empirical proof it works. Others claim to have spectacular results and have managed to eliminate long-standing fears, phobias and emotional distress after even just one EFT session. An article about EFT in The Huffington Post says there have been 17 studies published from 2008 to 2013 confirming the effectiveness of tapping and a number of medical professionals as well as the prestigious American Psychological Association have endorsed the legitimacy of EFT. Many top level professional athletes, celebrities and business people also tap for success.

If this is something that interests you then there are numerous videos and examples on You Tube. Just type in

"Tapping for confidence" or "EFT confidence" or even "Faster EFT self-confidence" into the search box and then follow along. It looks and feels strange to do it, but I have personally found it very effective, so why not have a go?

Anchoring Confidence

Neuro Linguistic Programming, known as NLP, is an umbrella term for a series of techniques and strategies to help improve your performance and transform your thinking and attitudes. It replaces negative thinking and limiting beliefs and thought patterns with models of excellence. NLP is very practical and apart from helping with specific issues, for example self-confidence, it teaches you how your mind works and what makes other people tick.

Neuro Linguistic Programming is quite a mouthful and the clue to the method is in the name. The "Neuro Linguistic" part refers to the use of language to program your own mind. It kind of talks to the mind in its own language. It is an excellent way to boost confidence, reduce anxiety and increase self-esteem. It also makes use of body language, including a technique to reinforce positive experiences known as anchoring.

NLP works very quickly and is not hard to learn. It is certainly worth adding to your toolkit of practical techniques, so let's take a closer look at some of the strategies. The anchoring one is very powerful.

- Think of one of your greatest achievements. Something you are very proud of. Close your eyes and go back to that moment.
- Relive it, how you felt, what people said, where you were.

- Think of one word to summarize your feelings.
- Think of a color you associate with this achievement.
- At the precise moment that the scene gets most vivid and intense, hold your right wrist with your left hand and say the word you chose, while seeing everything bathed in the color you chose. What you have just done is "anchored" the memory.

Anchors work using stimulus response, just like Pavlov's dogs, who salivated when they heard a bell ring because they associated it with food. You aren't going to be salivating, that would be weird, but you are going to start associating holding your right wrist with your left hand with strong, powerful feelings of achievement.

You can add to the stock of positive memories by repeating the exercise regularly and revisiting a different memory. You can also add any new achievements to the anchor when they happen, by touching your wrist at the time they happen. Now it's time to use the anchor you have established. Whenever you need a confidence or self-esteem boost grab your wrist and repeat the process and all those feelings of ability, pride and accomplishment will flood in.

Anchoring a specific state is something that must be used and topped up regularly, so make it part of your routine.

Tony Robbins – from Janitor to Billionaire Motivational Speaker
American author, entrepreneur and philanthropist Tony Robbins was one of the first people to popularize NLP after partnering with its founder John Grinder in the early 1980s.

Robbins came from an "abusive" and "chaotic" background. He worked as a janitor and handyman to help provide for his siblings and left home at the age of 17. He attended a self-help seminar by motivational speaker Jim Rohn and then worked promoting them. This was his introduction to the world of personal growth and he had found his calling. He became a "peak performance coach" and started to get celebrity clients.

Today, he is one of the biggest names in the industry and has worked with many household name clients like Bill Clinton, Serena Williams and Hugh Jackman. He is involved in 18 different businesses. About four million people have attended his live seminars. He is, by any measure, a big success (at 6 feet 7 inches he is also a big guy!) and whether you love him or loathe him, one of the most impressive aspects of his career is that he practices what he preaches. He focuses more than almost any trainer on a person's physiology and people who participate in his seminars are encouraged to go to their physical limits. He introduced fire-walking in his seminars back in the 1980s. He completely understands the mind body connection and the importance of techniques like anchoring.

You don't have to agree with Tony Robbins or follow his advice, but he is an excellent person to use as a model of supreme self-confidence.

Chapter 8 Key Take-Aways

In this chapter, we have looked at:

- The importance of tuning into your body.

- How to scan your body mentally and check how you really feel.

- A technique for using positive confident feelings and

anxious feelings as a barometer to evaluate situations and decisions.

- Emotional Freedom Technique and how to tap for confidence.

- Neuro Linguistic programming and anchoring success.

- How Tony Robbins is a good model to emulate.

Reconnecting with your body does a number of positive things. First of all, it makes you focus on the moment as you begin to pay attention to how you are feeling and then act on what you find.

It takes you out of your head and helps you appreciate your surroundings, getting back in touch with the earth and nature. It puts things in perspective and changes your outlook by boosting positive chemicals in your brain.

It helps balance your energy and build a stable and grounded foundation, both physically and mentally. Getting in touch with your feelings and responding to messages your body is giving you is a healthy and respectful way to treat yourself.

Having spent some time emphasizing the crucial part your physical body plays in building confidence, we're now going to move on to a different but vital area. We're going to study how the words that you speak and the conversations you have can influence how you feel and how others respond to you. Remember the saying *"sticks and stones can break my bones, but words will never hurt me?"* It is time to see if that is true!

Chapter 9 – Talking With Confidence In Any Situation

"Courage is what it takes to stand up and speak; courage is also what it takes to sit down and listen."
Winston Churchill

In this chapter, we are going to look at talking, and its associated and much underrated fellow skill, listening.

If you are shy and lack self-confidence then you will find making conversation very difficult, unless you feel totally relaxed with the person you're talking to. It's often hard to know what to talk about and how to keep a conversation going. Parties, or social gatherings where you're likely to meet new people, can be agonizing. Maybe you avoid those kind of occasions like the plague.

First, let me give you a word of reassurance. There is absolutely nothing wrong with liking your own company. Many people feel guilty if they are not as "sociable" as their friends, preferring a book to a bar outing. This is fine. I feel your pain, because I'm exactly the same. I don't enjoy small talk or crowds. I like my own company. I enjoy silence and tranquil settings over the hustle and bustle of large groups in city settings. But if I've got to, I can make great conversation and talk happily to people I have never met. I can switch on a "sociable me" and you would never know I would prefer to be in the woods with my dogs or curled up with a great novel.

Dealing with all types of social situations without batting an eyelid is a useful skill to have. Something that will stand you in good stead your whole life. It may not come naturally. You may wish you were halfway up a mountain conversing with a goat rather standing in your neighbor's yard talking to a man who looks like one, but you can do it if you need to.

The Conversation Dance

Dance? Oh yes. Not the kind of dance you do on your own, but the old-fashioned kind, maybe a waltz or a tango. The point is, in a conversation with another person, there are two parts. When you are feeling self-conscious, remember that. It isn't a monologue but a **dialogue**. And the old saying from Epictetus *"we have two ears and one mouth so that we can listen twice as much as we speak"*, is very true. It's really empowering to think that one of the most important things about being a great conversationalist is that you should be a great listener. Perfect the art of listening and people will think you are the best person they have ever had a conversation with!

Now, here's something to encourage you. Listening is something talkative, confident types are often not that good at. You see, if you are chatty and love center stage, you will only be listening just enough to see when you can next come in with your own great story.

Sometimes, chatty people get so excited about the really funny or witty thing they want to tell you that they literally bounce up and down, or say "yeah, yeah, yeah…" as you're talking. (Body language code for: "My turn, my turn!") The worst kind will just plain interrupt you with their own brilliant insights or how they have had it so much worse than you. This leaves the original speaker feeling annoyed or insignificant or insulted rather than entertained, but the show-off doesn't care as they hold forth with their own sparkling opinions, amazing anecdotes and dire tragedies.

So how do you listen well? It's more difficult to do this than to speak. If you're shy or lacking a bit in self-confidence then you have an advantage, because you're probably happy for the other person to do most of the talking. The only caveat is that you must genuinely listen. That means no multi-tasking and no other thoughts running through your mind, except what the person opposite to you is saying. If you are running an inner dialogue something along the lines of: *"oh no, what on earth can I say next? I don't know anything about this topic, they'll think I'm boring! Why did I come here? I should have stayed at home! I'd better think of an excuse and leave…"* then you are simply not giving them your full attention. You are as bad as the person who isn't listening because they can't wait to speak themselves.

Attentive listening means allowing some gaps in the dialogue, and not being embarrassed about them. Gaps give the other person time to think and speak again. Gaps are good.

Your body language is important. You need to have open body language (no arms or legs crossed) and to keep eye contact. Leaning forward rather than back shows you are involved and interested in what the other person is saying. Nodding or smiling (or laughing) when appropriate also enhances the rapport.

Although saying nothing while the other person is talking is often a good listening strategy, asking questions is sometimes very useful and encouraging. No, not questions like: *"have I told you about the time that very same thing happened to me?"* but questions which encourage the other person to speak more. Open-ended (who/how) questions are better than closed (yes/no) questions. Therefore, *"how did that make you feel?"* is a lot better than *"Did you feel upset?"*

You can also occasionally repeat back to someone what they have just said, but with a questioning tone, which encourages them to say more. Here's an example. You are B.

A: I'm having a lot of problems at work at the moment. It's driving me crazy!
B: Problems at work?

It's a fact that most people love talking about themselves, so if you are feeling shy and at a loss for what to say, asking some questions about your fellow conversationalist is a good strategy. Of course, this can make you sound like a job interviewer, so do intersperse this with some thoughts and opinions of your own. As with the good listening example above, open-ended questions are better as they allow the person more opportunity to give their opinion.

Here are some examples of conversation starter questions:
- What are you going to do this weekend?
- What did you do last weekend?
- How do you know … (the name of your party host or hostess)?
- What kind of food do you like?
- What book are you reading at the moment? What do you think of it?
- What personal goals do you have for the next year or so?
- What's your favorite time of day/day of the week/ season. Why?
- What's your favorite food? What do you like about it?

Often, it sounds more natural to talk a little about yourself first and then ask the question to the other person. Then you can follow up with another question and it doesn't sound too much like an interrogation! Here's an example using the last question from the list. You are "A":

A: I just love these little pizzas, but then Italian is my favorite food! What about you? Got a favorite?
B: I love anything hot, the hotter the better!

A: But if it's too hot you can't taste anything, can you?
B: Oh, you can! Even with chili peppers, they have different tastes, it's not just heat…

A: What kind of hot food do you like?
B: Hmm, I think it has to be Thai curry.

A: Thai curry? I'm not sure I've ever had that, what is it?

This sounds nice and natural. You are building the conversation on the responses of the other person and asking relevant, interesting questions. You can apply this technique to most conversation topics.

Confidence During Interviews

If you want to have more than one job in your life, (or any job in your life), then you will have to face being interviewed. If you are low in self-esteem or self-confidence then a job interview is a kind of purgatory for several reasons. Two of those are a) you are forced to talk about yourself and b) the attention is 100 percent on you. It's enough to give anyone the heebie-jeebies!

There are several things you can do to get through, and even excel at, an interview. One important thing is to understand what appropriate confidence looks like at an interview.

- You have a firm handshake.
- You look the interviewer(s) in the eye and smile where appropriate.
- You listen carefully and with attention to the questions you are asked.
- Your body language is open and strong (you are not curled in on yourself or sitting with your arms across your body).
- You speak calmly and not too fast.
- Your voice is audible, but not too loud.
- You ask questions if necessary.
- You connect with the interviewer (you want to build rapport, not show off).

Notice almost all those things are to do with body language rather than showing off your skills. People often think they are being judged at interview on how well you know your subject. Of course, a job interview is going to evaluate your ability to do a job, but more importantly, the interviewer is going to assess how well you will fit into their organization, how well you will get on with colleagues and how much of a team player you are. One organization I know includes as part of the assessment, but unknown to the candidate, the receptionist's opinion. Has the candidate been polite and friendly when they don't think they are "on show"? How do they deal with being told they need to wait a few minutes? (They've always got to wait a few minutes with this particular company – little do they know that it's part of the interview process!)

You can practice your body language and small talk skills with friends before the interview, because it is always good to be prepared. Also look on YouTube as there are plenty of videos about giving a good interview. Remember if you are interviewed and it goes well, then "anchor" it by holding your right wrist with your left hand, as we talked about in the previous chapter. Successes need to be celebrated and fixed in your memory.

Speaking in Public

A poll of over 2000 people about common phobias conducted by OnePoll in 2013 revealed a surprising statistic. More people were more afraid of public speaking than being buried alive. In case you are interested the name of this speaking fear is glossophobia. Catchy name eh?

Public speaking covers everything from giving a thank-you speech in front of six colleagues at an office leaving party to performing stand-up comedy on stage in front of thousands, (or millions if it's videoed.) It's definitely a scary thing to do, but scarier than dying? Well, apparently more than half of us think so.

It's comforting to know that even professionals get anxious before speaking in public. The thing is, their desire to do it overcomes their nerves. Many will tell you that the nerves don't go away, you just learn to deal with them. They'll also tell you that the more you speak in public, the easier it gets.

Now, unlike a professional comedian or speaker, most of us have only got to speak in public if we are forced to. It's one thing conquering your fears if you really love what you are doing and consider the trade-off of nerves for applause worth it. It's quite another if your boss has suddenly told you that you will be presenting the mid-quarter sales figures at the next meeting! So, are there any tips for handling a public speaking situation? Of course there are!

Practice, practice and then practice some more. If you are on your own, then practice in front of a mirror. If there is a friend to hand, then ask them to video you. The more comfortable you are with your material, the better. That means if you drop your notes, you won't be flustered because you already know the content. Be enthusiastic and express a good level of energy. That doesn't mean behaving like a maniac, but low energy and a dull, monotonous presentation is definitely not fun to listen to. Remember acting *"as if..."*? Well, act *as if* you are a confident and enthusiastic speaker.

Enthusiastic does **not** mean gabbling. Deliberately slow down your speech and allow time for pauses. When you're nervous you tend to do things much faster, including speaking. That's where a good amount of practice beforehand can really help. Once you are happy about what you are going to say, then spend time on speaking slowly and in not too high a pitch, and on building in a few key pauses.

Watch speeches and presentations given by confident people (for example, Brian Tracy). Turn the sound down and just watch them. How do they move? How do they hold their arms and hands? Where do they look? How is their posture? How about their facial expressions?

Do not be afraid to tell people that you feel nervous! As we have seen, most people are scared of doing what you're doing, so they'll empathize. But don't get too apologetic and self-deprecating. It sets a negative tone and is quite tedious to listen to. One brief comment about feeling nervous at the start is fine.

Keep your sentences short. Politicians use the trick of *"talking in threes"*, so they have three parts to an idea or they repeat the same phrase three times. For example: *"I don't want to talk to you about work. I don't want to talk to you about money. I don't want to talk to you about love. What I'm going to tell you is far more important than that…"*

Pick a subject you really care about. (Assuming you have that option.) People will forgive anything if they see how passionate you are. Emotions are good. You can distract yourself from feeling nervous if you are speaking about something that makes you angry, happy, excited, sad and so on. In general, people prefer a presentation with a personal touch that engages their emotions than something which relies on too much information or data.

Focus on one or two sympathetic looking people in the audience (those who are smiling or nodding in the right places) and deliver the speech to them.

If you can make people laugh then you will have won their hearts. It can even be good to have a joke ready in case you make a mistake. But don't overdo it. You're not auditioning for stand-up.

How Warren Buffet Conquered His Public Speaking Nerves

Warren Buffet is an American investor, businessman, philanthropist and speaker. Born in 1930, he is something of a legend. As of August 2017, he is the second wealthiest person in the United States and the fourth wealthiest in the world with a total net worth of $73.3 billion. Buffet is, in anyone's book, a very successful man. Yet as a young man, this financial giant used to be so terrified of speaking in public he would literally throw up before addressing an audience. At college, Buffet was so petrified he might have to get up and talk in front of his fellow students that he only chose classes where this would not happen. He signed up for a course on public speaking but was too terrified to even begin it. Quite a problem, I'm sure you'll agree.

The first positive thing that Buffet did to address his phobia was to acknowledge it. He admitted that it was an issue for him. The second important thing he did was to make the decision to do something about it. He was very aware that if he wanted to have a successful career, he would have to overcome his fear of speaking in public. In an interview on a website for young women Levo League, he said: *"You've got to be able to communicate in life and it's enormously important. Schools, to some extent, underemphasize that. If you can't communicate and talk to other people and get across your ideas, you're giving up your potential."*

Buffet once again enrolled for a public speaking course, but this time he saw it through. The Dale Carnegie course changed his life, although he didn't find it easy. He describes how he and his 30 fellow participants: *"... were all just terrified. We couldn't say our own names. We all stood there and wouldn't talk to each other."*

The students were each given a book of example speeches and had to present one a week. Gradually, he improved. The students all helped and encouraged each other. Although he learned a few tips and ways to overcome his nerves, he is also sure that one of the most important factors was simply doing it. *"Some of it is just practice, just doing it and practicing. And it worked. That's the most important degree I have."*

Today Warren Buffet is as relaxed and comfortable in front

of the mic as behind it. He was so right to invest in that public speaking course! Working on your speaking skills won't necessarily turn you into a business guru and wildly successful investor like Warren Buffet. But investing the time and energy into your own confidence skills will pay dividends in myriad other ways.

Chapter 9 Key Take-Aways

In this chapter, we have looked at:

- How it's OK to enjoy your own company, as long as you can also function well in social situations.

- How a conversation is like a dance, with both people being equally important.

- The importance of listening well and how this is something that a shy person can excel at.

- Using questions as a way of opening or deepening a conversation.

- How to behave confidently at interview.

- The very common fear of public speaking and some tips and techniques for overcoming it.

- How billionaire Warren Buffet overcame his speaking phobia.

We've almost reached the end of this short guide to building confidence, so well done for still being here. In the final chapter, we're going to look at a very important area – relating to other people. It doesn't matter if it's at work, at home, with friends or with strangers, you need to express your opinions, wants and needs confidently and with just the right degree of assertiveness. So, let's complete this last stage of our journey together. Are you ready?

Chapter 10 - Relating To Others With Ease And Confidence

"When dealing with people, remember you are not dealing with creatures of logic, but creatures of emotion."
Dale Carnegie

All of us, unless we are hermits, encounter other people on a regular basis and build different relationships with them. Even if you are a solitary type by nature, research has shown that spending quality time with others is good for you. Apparently, you are 50 percent more likely to live longer if you have healthy relationships, so maybe it's time to put down your book and pick up the phone! You can usually divide relationships into three main groups: personal relationships (partners, friends and family), professional relationships (work colleagues, other professionals and clients) and relationships with vague acquaintances and strangers.

A self-confident, but not over-confident, approach is the key to success in all three kinds of relationship. In personal relationships, a good level of self-confidence and self-esteem (remember, the first is external and the second is internal) can help you deal with any criticism and negativity. It lets you see where someone is being genuinely helpful and caring and where they are being abusive or manipulative.

In business and professional relationships, self-confidence allows you to accept challenges, take calculated risks and show leadership. It also means you can stand up for yourself if necessary and know your own worth. Clients and colleagues usually respond well to a confident approach and someone who believes in what they are doing and shows it.

When dealing with the rest of the world – that is, vague acquaintances and strangers – a self-confident person with a smile and a kind heart will be able to deal with most situations. You never know what the world is going to throw at you, good or bad, and in your lifetime, you will have to deal with many different kinds of situation involving people you don't know. If you have a healthy level of self-esteem then you assume that most people will usually treat you fairly. And if they don't, you know that it isn't personal. On the other hand, if you suffer from low self-esteem, you might think everyone is out to criticize you or make a fool of you and that you don't blame them as you probably deserve it. It may cause you to treat strangers with suspicion or dislike, even if they have done nothing wrong and that can cause all kinds of repercussions which help reinforce your negative impression of them.

It's useful to remember that most people are only really interested in **themselves**. Despite how it may feel, they aren't all looking at you, thinking about you or really that bothered by what you do. The old motto *"do as you would be done by"*, that is, treating someone as you would like to be treated yourself, is a good one to follow. That involves developing a certain amount of empathy for your fellow humans.

Emotional Intelligence

The ability to recognize, understand and manage your own emotions and those of other people is often referred to as Emotional Intelligence. The concept was only fully developed in the 1990s so is relatively recent.

The correct short form for emotional intelligence is **EI**, but it is popularly and internationally referred to as **EQ**, a play on the famous intelligence measurement known as IQ. Once upon a time, not that long ago, a high IQ was considered one of the most desirable things you could have. But in our more enlightened times we understand that intelligence without emotional skills can be more of a handicap than a blessing.

Although you can have a high or low score on both, there is no correlation between IQ and EQ. It is perfectly possible to be a highly intelligent academic with terrible "people skills" and I'm sure we can all think of examples from our own experience. The reverse is true and you have people who don't score highly on IQ tests and yet they are brilliant at dealing with and understanding the emotions of others.

There are various ways to measure EQ, which we will look at in a minute, but one thing is for sure. A high level of emotional intelligence (a high EQ) is a positive thing to have. It helps you understand your own emotional state and employ techniques to manage it. People with a high EQ are less likely to suffer from depression or chronic stress. People with a high EQ are also better able to handle relationships, whether with individuals or groups.

What's Your EQ?

Take a few moments to look at each of the below statements and then give each one a score from 1 to 5.

Scoring system:
1 = strongly disagree
2 = disagree
3 = neither agree nor disagree

4 = agree
5 = strongly agree

Appraisal of own emotions:
1 - I a fully aware and know why my emotions change.
2 - I easily recognize my own emotions as I experience them.

Appraisal of others' emotions:
3 - I can tell how people are feeling simply by listening to the tone of their voice.
4 - I recognize the emotions people are experiencing when I look at peoples facial expressions.

Regulation of own emotions:
5 - I look for activities that make me happy.
6 - I have control over my own emotions.

Regulation of others' emotions:
7 - I arrange situations that other people seem to enjoy.
8 - I help people feel better when they are down.

Utilization of emotions:
9 - When I am in a positive mood, I am able to figure out new ideas.
10 - I use my good and positive mood to help myself keep trying in the face of challenges.

What your score means.
This is quite straightforward. The higher your score the higher your EQ. And when it comes to EQ, the higher the better! What is interesting is that the questions are divided into various areas, so you may find that you score highly on understanding and regulating your own emotions, but not so highly on doing the same for other people.

How to Develop Emotional Intelligence

The good think about emotional intelligence, is that you can develop and improve it if you practice. Here are some exercises to try. There are lots more ideas online if you just Google *"how to develop emotional intelligence"* for example.

Develop Mindfulness

In the last chapter, we looked at the importance of scanning your body regularly and really tuning in to how you feel physically. Well, do the same with your emotions. Take regular "time-outs" to identify your emotions at that specific time. Try and name the emotion if you can and see how it manifests itself. Bear in mind an emotion could have a physical feeling connected with it. You might find that feeling happy creates a warm glow in your chest or midriff, for example, or makes you smile.

When you feel particular emotions, try and identify why you are feeling them. What triggered the reaction? A comment? A smell? A song? Once you have identified a trigger, think about whether this always produces the same emotional reaction.

Once you have identified a specific emotion yourself, ask other people what emotion they think you are feeling and why they think that. This will show you how other people perceive your behavior. Don't be surprised if this has some unexpected results. You may be feeling really happy, yet a friend thinks you are bored. What body language message are you sending out that would make them say that? If you think it's important, then could you change it? How?

Ask close friends and family members if they would mind discussing recent situation (positive or negative) that involved you both. Ask them if they thought you understood their point of view? Why or why not? Did they think you were sensitive and understanding? Ask them exactly how they were feeling and why they felt that. Warning! Don't turn this into an opportunity to relive an argument or give your opinion. You are listening and learning. Again, you might be surprised by what you discover.

Count to Ten. Yes, our parents or grandparents were probably right when they said, *"count to ten and take a deep breath before you answer."* They weren't getting us to practice our math. What counting to ten does is give us time to reflect before we dive into a situation headfirst or say something we might regret.

Confidence in Your Romantic Life

When it comes to romance, many people just completely lose the plot. Others never lose their good level of self-esteem. I remember my amazing mother telling me how, as a young woman, she saw a guy she had been out on a couple of dates was chatting up another girl, although he didn't know my mother had seen him. *"That was the end of him,"* she said with a laugh. *"He kept phoning me up, begging for a date. He was completely baffled at my reaction and I didn't tell him the reason why either. But I never went out with him again. I respected myself far too much."*

That may be quite a drastic reaction, but my mother was showing a high level of self-esteem and was simply not prepared to be anyone's second best option. She had her values and she stuck to them. (And incidentally this paid off, as she eventually married my wonderful father who always treated her like a queen!)

To look at celebrity websites and magazines, you would think that looks are everything in a relationship, but dig a little deeper and you'll find this simply doesn't hold water. There are some extremely beautiful or handsome celebs out there who have serial marriages and tragic love lives. They're pretty, but people still treat them badly and leave them. What does that tell you? To have a solid, loving and caring intimate relationship with another person is something we all crave. It isn't a pipe dream. It is achievable if you have the confidence to be yourself and the confidence to let the other person be themselves too.

The **real** you is the **only** you that should show up on a date. Of course, you can get dressed up and made up, looking your best is fun and a sign of respect for the person you're with (who wants to go out with someone who looks like they've just crawled off the couch and out the door?), but don't "make up" your personality as well. You are more than good enough as you are. You don't have to pretend to be something you're not. You don't have to fake interest in baseball or Beethoven because the target of your affections happens to love them. Because it may work short term, but after a few months or years, you won't be able to hide what you really feel about the next Red Sox game or the German composer's fifth symphony.

Confidence is attractive. I cannot repeat that enough! Be proud of who you are, what you like and what you dislike. Don't let yourself think that they are only going out with you from desperation and they are bound to find someone better soon. Be like my mom, don't put up with any crap.

You deserve to be treated well, so set some boundaries and stick to them. If exclusivity is what you want, then make that clear, but in an empowering way. So, don't say: *"If I find out you're dating other women I will never speak to you again and this relationship will be over!"* That sounds like a threat and also quite needy. Try: *"You're perfectly entitled to see other women while you're dating me, but that's not what I'm looking for in a relationship."* Stating your needs is always a strong and independent thing to do, so long as it is done in a non-threatening and non-aggressive way. I know you will be afraid that the person will walk away and the relationship will be over, but better to find that out now than in the future when you have got more involved.

If you find that you are constantly projecting into the future, or dwelling on the past then you are not going to have a fulfilling and enjoyable relationship with anyone, romantic or not. We all have a tendency to imagine scenarios and fast forward ourselves into a dream future - or a nightmare one, if you are always imagining things are going to end badly. The problem with this kind of behavior is that it stops you fully enjoying the only real time you ever have - the now. Living fully in the moment, savoring every sight, sound and sensation is a good way to enjoy the company of your partner and take your mind off what may or may not happen down the line.

Confidence at Work

"You wouldn't worry so much about what others think of you if you realized how seldom they do."
Eleanor Roosevelt

It is basic common sense that confident people with healthy self-esteem are respected and listened to at work and tend to be happier and do better than those who have low levels of self-esteem and confidence. But what can you do if you are more shrinking violet than dazzling sunflower?

One of the best ways to build confidence at work is to know yourself inside out. It means identifying your strengths and weaknesses, talents and skills. In that way, you can focus on projects and ideas that showcase your abilities and bring you tons of kudos when you do them well. This sounds so obvious, but it is quite surprising how many people will spend their time doing things that they don't excel at.

Although you can work on weaknesses, it's probably better to focus on being the very best at the things you are naturally good at. Ignoring your weaknesses doesn't come easy though. As research done in 2016 by psychologists Andreas Steiner and André Mata has proved, *"people perceive their weaknesses as more malleable than their strengths."* In other words, people think that it is easier to change a weakness than change a strength, which is one reason they may choose to try and work on things they are not so good at. The general work environment is also traditionally more weighted towards pointing out problems than praising excellence. If you have a performance evaluation, it probably highlights several areas that could do with improvement, because many supervisors feel it is their duty to point out your flaws. But if you think about it, this doesn't make sense and isn't a good use of your resources. Instead of spending precious time and energy going from mediocre to average in a skill, why not spend it on moving from above average to outstanding?

As with any other area of confidence, at work it pays to

plan, practice and prepare. Put on the outfit that makes you feel great, remember your previous successes using the NLP anchor technique and make sure you know your material well if you need to do a presentation. Remember to revel in your expertise, because time spent becoming the best at what you are naturally strong at means you will be more knowledgeable and capable than most of the other people around you, which is an automatic confidence booster.

If you are feeling a little shaky, then remember the technique of acting "as if". Imagine you are the best in your field, the top of your game. How would they do the thing you are a bit scared about? Use body language to present a positive and enthusiastic image. Stand up straight, put your shoulders back. Smile and "act confident". And remember, if things go a little wrong, it's not the end of the world. As an ex-military friend of mine is fond of saying, *"it's not that bad, nobody's shooting at you."* That kind of puts things in perspective, doesn't it?

Being Assertive In Any Situation

In any kind of relationship, personal or professional, you need to be able to draw boundaries, express your point of view and speak up for your needs and those of others. Unfortunately, many of are only used to doing this in a confrontational situation, where we yell and scream and the other person does the same. This makes us feel that we can only disagree with someone or express strong opinions if it is part of an argument. As a result, we decide to let things ride rather than cause a scene. We tell ourselves we are relaxed and easygoing, that nothing bothers us and we just go with the flow when the truth is that we are just acting that way. Inwardly we are seething and resentful.

Let's get something straight. You don't have to be angry to state your needs and views. You don't have to raise your voice, cry, bang your fist on the table or fall out with the person or people you're talking to. Assertion does not equal aggression. It doesn't mean you are not a nice person. It means you are confident enough not to be walked all over. It means you think highly enough of yourself that you will not let unreasonable behavior pass. It means being honest and direct.

Being assertive is an interpersonal skill, and an important one too. Like any skill it can be learned and it takes practice to get good at it. Making the decision to be more assertive can be hard, because it's always easier to stick with situations you feel comfortable in than make boundary-stretching scary changes.

Here are some ways to practice being assertive:

Set boundaries.
Know your values and the things that are important to you, in all areas of your life: family, faith, work, politics, health and so on. If you don't know these, or haven't thought about them then you should do, so take some time out and get your head straight on these. Decide on your limits and boundaries and then stick to them. If, for example, your health boundaries mean that you are against smoking in your home, then don't let big bully cousin Dwayne do it in your house, even if he usually ignores you and lights up anyway and is likely to argue back loudly about his rights. Your home, your rules. If your date wants sex on the first night and your boundaries say no, then don't cave in just because they might think you are a prude and not want to see you again. Your body, your rules.

State what you want calmly and clearly.

People are not mind readers, they will not magically "know" that you are unhappy with a situation unless you speak up. Part of being assertive is owning what you say and what you think. Note the calm and clear part. Just because you are disagreeing with something or someone, it doesn't mean you need to argue or get emotional. Just state your case. That's it.

Accept there may be some fallout. Some people don't like to be contradicted. Others may resent the former passive you suddenly having opinions and boundaries. They may shout and scream. That doesn't mean you need to. It may not be nice, but you must learn to allow a level of discomfort as you state your feelings. Better that than be walked all over for the rest of your life.

Know that you are not responsible for the reactions and opinions of others.

So long as you have not been cruel, mean, thoughtless or heartless, then you are allowed to say what you think, you are allowed to contradict or disagree. Don't be afraid that people won't like you if you speak up. If someone is upset about your opinion or point of view, that is their problem, not yours. Don't feel guilty about someone else's reaction.

Rosa Parks – Quiet Strength

This small, softly-spoken and sweet lady was the kind you would pass by in the street and hardly notice. Yet Rosa Parks had clear values and principles and her name has gone down in history as the woman who, in December 1955, refused to obey Alabama bus driver James F. Blake's order to give up her seat to a white passenger on a bus when all the whites-only section seats were taken.

Although she wasn't the first person to refuse to participate in bus segregation, she became an icon for the American

Civil Rights Movement.

Rosa Parks' protest was not loud, angry and aggressive. She demonstrated the very best kind of assertive behavior. Douglas Brinkley's biography of her, written in 2000, describes what happened: *"Are you going to stand up?"* the driver demanded. Rosa Parks looked straight at him and said: *"No."* Flustered, and not quite sure what to do, Blake retorted, *"Well, I'm going to have you arrested."* And Parks, still sitting next to the window, replied softly, *"You may do that."*

She was arrested and fined $10. She had clearly expressed her views and calmly stayed put. This tiny lady didn't do what her fellow African American passengers did. She had the courage of her convictions and in showing assertiveness, she changed American history.

Chapter 10 Key Take-Aways

In this chapter, we have looked at:

- Three different types of interpersonal relationship.

- How confidence is the key to success in all three types.

- Emotional Intelligence, (known as EQ or EI) what it is and how you rate.

- Ways to develop EQ.

- The importance of confidence in your intimate relationships.

- How to act confidently in a professional situation.

- Assertiveness and how to develop a healthy level of it.

- The story of Rosa Parks and her quiet assertiveness.

By developing confidence in your interpersonal relationships and using the right degree of assertiveness you may not change the lives of millions like Rosa Parks, but you will most certainly change your own and those of the people around you in a positive way. And that has got to be good.

It's almost time to say goodbye. But before we do, let's evaluate everything we've looked at together. It's time for me to conclude and for you to begin.

The Time To Live With Confidence Is Now

This book began with a Rose, the character shy actress Kate Winslet played in Titanic, and ended with a Rosa, Rosa Parks, the quietly brave lady who became a figurehead for the Civil Rights movement in the USA. I didn't intend it like that, but these things take on a life of their own and unexpectedly the roses metaphor has happened. So, I want to explore it in this conclusion. I don't know where it will lead, but in our journey towards self-confidence and self-esteem, I am sure that there is an energy and a message there for us all.

The rose is a symbol of rebirth, renewal and balance. Its many layers slowly unfold to reveal its true wonder. In many religions, the rose represents something miraculous. It is almost universally acknowledged to represent timeless beauty and love.

I feel the message of the rose in this book is no coincidence. In giving yourself the gift of self-confidence and self-esteem, you are allowing your true self to flower, your true beauty to come out. Just as the rose takes time to form, bud and flower, it will take time for you to practice what you have learned and see the results, but you will see them.

A rose has no choice but to follow its life cycle through the various stages. It doesn't let anything get in the way. Look at the wild roses in nature, pushing their way through old walls and abandoned roads, determined to bring beauty wherever they go. They grow despite torrential rain and scorching sun. Their job is to be a rose and that is what they do.

And that is what you must do now. Push through the difficulties and **keep going**. Work on your self-confidence, because there is no-one in the world quite like you and you deserve to be heard and to do the work you were put on this earth to do. No-one can do it for you, it's your decision, but it will be life-changing if you decide to do it. Many people will benefit from the new, more confident self you present to the world. I hope this book will, in some small way, help you do that.

Now, it's over to you. Be like the rose and let your true beauty shine.

"If the rose is a beautiful flower, it is also because it opens itself."
Charles de Leusse

If You Have Time, Could You Do Me A Favor?

Thank you so much for checking out my book.

I sincerely hope you got value from it. I hope it allows you to make important changes in your life. I hope this book helps you increase your self-confidence, assertiveness and self- esteem, but most of all your happiness.

If you liked this book could you possibly taking 60 seconds to write a quick review about this book on Amazon?

Reviews are a vital way for books to get more exposure and help to spread the message. Thank you. Your support is very much appreciated.

Michelle Gates

Printed in Great Britain
by Amazon

85447820R00078